The Wise Child

* * *

OTHER BOOKS BY SONIA CHOQUETTE

The Psychic Pathway
Your Heart's Desire

The Wise Child

A Spiritual Guide to Nurturing Your Child's Intuition

✳ ✳ ✳

SONIA CHOQUETTE, PH.D.

Three Rivers Press
New York

Published by Three Rivers Press, a division of Crown Publishers, Inc., 201 East 50th Street, New York, New York 10022. Member of the Crown Publishing Group.

Random House, Inc. New York, Toronto, London, Sydney, Auckland
www.randomhouse.com

THREE RIVERS PRESS is a registered trademark of Random House, Inc.

Printed in the United States of America

Design by Jane Treuhaft

Library of Congress Cataloging-in-Publication Data
Choquette, Sonia.
    The wise child : a spiritual guide to nurturing your child's
intuition / by Sonia Choquette. — 1st ed.
    1. Intuition (Psychology)   2. Child rearing.   I. Title.
BF315.5C48   1999
649'.1—dc21   98-38273

ISBN 0-609-80399-9

10 9 8 7 6 5 4 3 2 1

First Edition

To my precious daughters, Sonia and Sabrina.
Thank you for the gift of your delightful spirits,
your wise insights, your endless sense of humor,
your honesty, and your profoundly generous,
forgiving, and loving hearts. It is my greatest joy
in life to be your mother.

✳ ✳ ✳

And to my mother, who taught me to see
what is true in life. I shall be forever grateful
for the gifts you have given me.

Acknowledgments

I would like to thank my parents, Sonia and Paul, for living the greatest love story of all time. You have shown me the wisdom of following my heart and shown me how loved and safe I really am. You'll never know how much I love and appreciate you both.

To my beloved husband and partner, Patrick Tully. Thank you for the gift of our precious daughters and for being a true heart-based and present father. You have provided a circle of safety, protection, and love that has allowed us to venture into the unknown with confidence. Thank you for believing in me and for teaching me the importance of the small daily nurturings of life. My adventure with you has been truly a banquet of delights.

To Carol Southern, my editor. Thank you for the monumental effort it took on your part to transform my manuscript into a completed book. I am eternally grateful for your mastery and patience in helping me bring this project to fruition. Thanks for not giving up.

To Kathy Churay, dear friend and lifesaver. Thank you for so diligently working on my behalf, turning a mountain of scribbled papers into a manuscript, while never once making me feel guilty.

To my mentor and soul sister, Lu Ann Glatzmaier. Thank you for being my teacher, my counselor, and the best and most precious of friends. And for listening to my worries when you have enough of your own.

To Joan Smith. You are, without a doubt in my mind, Saint Joan. Thank you for charting my course, month by month, advising me through the most difficult periods while writing this book. Without your direction and encouragement, I am certain I would have lost my way.

To my second mom, my sister Cuky. Thank you for the care and time you gave me, Patrick, Sonia, and Sabrina during this past year. You kept us all from having psychic overload and renewed our weary souls. You teach me the meaning of kindness toward self.

To the Hoffman Institute. Thank you for taking me back to my essence once again and liberating me from all the psychic debris of living in the ordinary world. And especially to you, Anne Simon-Wolf. You healed my spirit.

To Julia Cameron, my dear friend and writing mentor. Thank you for untangling my confusion and setting me on the right course at a time when you were so overloaded, you didn't have a minute to spare.

To my marvelous agent and friend, Susan Schulman. Thank you for believing in this project and taking it to the world without hesitation and especially for finding it such a wonderful home. Once again you have proven that you are the best.

To Lauren Shakely, and Chip Gibson, and all the people at Crown who have provided a wonderful home for all of my books, and especially for believing in this project, the most dear of all to my own heart.

To my teachers Charlie Goodman and Dr. Trenton Tully and my clients and students who have served as inspiration in my work. Most of all, to the children of the Universe. You are the real teachers of truth. I humbly thank and honor you.

Contents

And now here is my secret, a very simple secret: it is only with the heart that one can see rightly; what is essential is invisible to the eye.

—ANTOINE DE SAINT-EXUPÉRY

Introduction

I live in a large and sunny house on a tree-lined street in Chicago. I share the house with my husband, Patrick; my two daughters, Sonia and Sabrina; our dog, Miss T; and a steady stream of clients who come to see me in my role as intuitive counselor. Every day I sit in my office, amid my books and spiritual talismans, and listen to people as they ask me about their deepest dreams and desires. Often I feel that the room is crowded with far more than the presence of my client and me—entire families seem to stand in the wings, because the deepest dreams for many people concern the well-being and happiness of those they love.

"How can I help my children to thrive and prosper?" I am often asked. "How can I teach my children to trust themselves so they won't become unhappy or frustrated as I have been? How can I protect them and give them the skills they need to be the best that they can be?"

"Children learn by what we do," I tell my clients gently. "If you want your children to thrive as happy and well-integrated beings, you must show them how. You must create an environment in your home that honors their fullest flowering. You must recognize that they, like you, are spiritual beings, and as such they have a direct connection to the loving Source of all wisdom. This connection is experienced as a 'sixth sense,' their intuition. You must develop and honor their intuition if you are to raise what I call a wise child."

"But Sonia, how do I do that?"

"Step by step," I answer. "You must awaken in your children a sense of their soulful heritage, and provide them with an atmosphere of spiritual safety and well-being in the home. This sense begins by creating that spiritual awareness and atmosphere within yourself. As a parent you set the tone for their intuitive awakening. You are the source from which your children take their cues. An intuitively awakened and spiritually integrated parent who has a strong connection to his or her own inner guidance and well-being makes it possible for that same sense to flourish in a child."

"Sonia, that sounds impossible to me! How did you learn to be so intuitively connected? How did you come to recognize and embrace so completely your inner voice and then pass this wisdom on to your family?"

People wonder whether I was born with a special gift or whether I had some mystical experience at an early age—whether it's simply a case of "either you've got it or you don't."

"We're all intuitive because we are all spiritual beings," I tell my clients. "Intuition is our heart-based connection to our Inner Teacher, the guiding voice of our soul. The difference is that I was brought up knowing this. In my case, the most significant and influential factor in developing a strong intuition was the mother I had, as well as a family environment that not only allowed for intuition, but actually *centered* on it."

Let me take a moment and talk to you about my own mother.

MY MOTHER'S STORY

My mother, the Sonia for whom I was named, was born in Romania to an artistic and religious mother and a sensual and passionate father. The second to the youngest of ten children, she lived a life of comfort and privilege in a country setting, where her father produced wine. My mother recalls that both her parents had very strong intuition. My grandmother, a religious woman, prayed openly for divine guidance and freely acknowledged the constant flow of intuitive direction she received in all matters. Her relationship to God was one of feeling loved and protected, a feeling she passed on to her children. My grandfather, a practical man, would wheel and deal with the townspeople, making decisions according to his gut instincts. His instincts were reliable, a fact he celebrated openly, and the family prospered. Through her parents my mother learned that inner guidance was available for the asking, and following her inner voice was the best way to direct her life. Her connection to spirit's wisdom was organic and intimate. It became second nature to her. But my mother's idyllic life changed abruptly in the fall of 1943, when she was twelve years old. War had broken out in Europe, and one day she and her entire family, along with thousands of others in her town, were evacuated from their homes to avoid bombardment by the invading Germans. In the confusion my mother was accidentally separated from her family during an air raid. She was lucky to survive the bombing, but along with hundreds of other refugees she was driven from the fields and rounded up as a prisoner. She and the other refugees were forced to march for days into Germany, where they were put into a POW camp.

My mother told me that at this time of danger and crisis, when she was completely cut off from her family and safety, she found herself faced with a decision: she could either look outward into a sea of terror or turn inward for direction. For her, the choice was simple. She did what she had seen her parents do in a million subtle ways. With nothing to grasp on to she turned inward for help and found that her intuition kicked in with full force.

In my mother's case, intuition became her lifeline to survival. Without anyone to care for or protect her, and in the most extreme conditions of war, her inner voice consoled, grounded, and ultimately liberated her. When people around her were despairing and dying, something inside her fought back. An inner compass kept her focused on living. Its vigilant counsel was, "Look. Listen. Be aware! Stay calm!" and whenever she feared death, her inner voice would assure her, "No, not now. Not you." My mother said that it might just have been her fierce desire to survive, but her inner voice became her constant and beloved companion. And somehow, through its counsel, she always managed to escape, often narrowly, mass executions, starvation, and even death by despair.

The spring my mother was fourteen, soldiers in her camp began separating the prisoners, and she was shunted off with those to be sent to Odessa, Russia, where she knew that women were raped, tortured, and left to die. Panic welled up in her, but almost instantly it was contained by the assurance of her inner voice once again saying, "No. Not this, either." But in spite of her intuition she was put on the Odessa train along with several hundred other prisoners.

As the train was pulling out of the station and gathering speed, my mother found herself in front of an open boxcar door. No one seemed to notice her. Like a shot her intuition shouted, "Now! Jump!" and the intensity of it literally *pushed* her out the train door. She leapt into the air, thinking that even death by falling would be less painful than what awaited her in Russia.

Before she could even complete the thought she hit the ground and rolled safely to a stop in a grassy field. She lay there for hours without moving before she dared even to test her arms and legs. Amazingly, not a bone was broken. Once again her inner counsel had saved her.

She lay in the field for several days, but eventually, weak with hunger and fatigue, she walked into a nearby village and turned herself in to local townspeople. Initially a farmer's wife took pity on her and hid her in a barn, offering her what little food she could. But as my mother later said, in many ways the villagers too were prisoners of the insanity of war, and eventually the family, fearing repercussions for hiding my mother, took her back to the local military authorities of the camp.

By this time, however, the soldiers seemed less interested in dealing with her and instead were only annoyed by the nuisance in the face of much larger problems. They put her in the kitchen of the Nazi general's headquarters and told her to help the cook. It was a miracle. She was safe, sound, and even managed occasionally to get a bit more than gruel for supper. Even so, she weighed only about sixty pounds.

A year and a half later the tide of war turned. Suddenly the Americans descended upon the town, took over the headquarters, and liberated thousands of prisoners from the camps. My mother found herself on her own in the small Bavarian village of Dingolfing, living above a stable with another young liberated Hungarian girl. The name of the game at that point was survival of the fittest. Her inner voice took on a new and urgent role: "Find food!"

My mother's remarkable spirit accepted the challenge, and the hunt was on. She learned to collect cigarette butts and reroll them into cigarettes, two of them worth a single egg or potato. She learned to gather wood, milk cows, sew, needlepoint, scrub dishes—whatever it took to scrape together a morsel of this or that. She wore cast-off army boots and an old sweater. She wrapped rags around her legs to keep warm. As she later told me, "It was a time of being at our very best creative incentive."

Even after the liberation, despair prevailed among the survivors, who, like my mother were displaced from home, with no way to connect with their families, with no resources and no one in war-ravaged Germany to help them. But not my mother. Intuition all the while cheering her on, she felt certain that she would be all right.

"Perhaps it was youth, innocence, and naïveté," she says, "perhaps it was denial on a monumental level, but never once would my intuition let me think about what could happen to me. It just urged me on, assuring me all the while to keep going, day by day."

The liberating American soldiers set up temporary law and order in the towns and villages of Germany, and in the fall of 1945 a young, handsome American soldier named Paul arrived in Dingolfing. Every young girl admired him because he was so good-looking and of course because he was known in town as "the Big Cheese." Once again my mother's inner voice had something to say about things. "He's the one for you," it said, and she agreed.

One day she told her girlfriend about her intuition. The friend laughed out loud and said, "Sonia, the war must have scrambled your senses. Have you seen yourself lately? With so many blond German girls in clean, beautiful clothes, all dying to meet him, why would he ever give somebody like you the time of day? I admire your optimism, but you're surely going too far!"

This angered my mother, and for the first time since her whole ordeal began she started to doubt her inner voice. It shook her considerably. After all, the inner guidance was all she had to keep her alive. She retorted, "You're wrong! I am somebody!" and walked away, shaken and depressed.

As time passed my mother continued to admire the handsome sergeant who sped around the town and countryside in his jeep. But he never once looked up and noticed her. Perhaps her friend was right, she thought. Perhaps her inner voice was betraying her.

One spring day she was walking back to the village, carrying two loads of firewood to the local *gasthaus* in exchange for a bowl of soup, when she noticed the soldier's jeep approaching at a fast clip. She stopped to watch him and smiled her biggest smile. He ignored her and sped past, driving through a huge mud puddle and drenching her from head to toe. She was furious. What an insult!

She dropped her bundle and ran after his jeep, yelling with fury. He must have heard or sensed her, because he looked into his rearview mirror and saw her covered with mud, waving her arms and screaming in a strange language. He stopped the jeep and turned back to apologize and help her, and the following year the dashing Sergeant Paul Choquette married my sixteen-year-old mother and brought her to America, where they settled in Denver and raised seven children. I came along, the second girl, and was named after my spunky mother.

My mother gave us the best she had to give, the best her mother and father had given her. She didn't have much education at the time, but she did have wisdom, and that wisdom became the heartbeat of our family. She gave us the message that no matter what we would face in life, no matter what challenges or obstacles, if we turned inward to our hearts instead of allowing outward circumstances to overwhelm us, if we recognized and focused on our deep spiritual connection to the Universe, to God—then we would be guided and protected, because that is the natural plan. The Universe would unquestionably show us what to do, where to go, how to thrive, as it had for her.

Our family's code word for this inner compass was "vibes," because that's what intuition felt like—a subtle, vibrating energy that centered in the heart and moved outward to the stomach, the gut, the chest, the throat. Like waves of direction getting our attention as if to say, "Do this," "Go there," "Avoid that," vibes ruled our lives. We navigated by them as birds navigate by sound. Intuitive knowing arrives via energy— some form of elusive energy, guiding, leading, and directing—and being aware of this energy was the way we were taught to lead our lives.

In my family, the inner voice was not the sixth sense. It was the first sense, the primary sense to focus on. Situations and options were tried on like shoes, and we were asked by our mother, and eventually by ourselves, "How does this feel, energetically? Does it feel right? Does it fit? Does it feel safe, secure, and comfortable? Will it support us and provide what we really need?" If we could feel and say "yes," we were assured that was the safe and correct way to go. If ever we felt "no," that the vibes felt uncomfortable, then we had the freedom to say so, and my mother would respect and even defend our feelings—no matter what the consequences. Each one of us grew up with a very strong, clear, and confident connection to our spiritual essence and our intuitive knowing.

HOW THIS APPLIES TO YOU

People ask me whether my intuition is a gift, and I have come to answer "yes." But mine was not the gift of being endowed with an "extra sense." The gift was having a mother who created a spiritual awareness and an environment for me that encouraged *all* my senses to develop. In my case, and that of my siblings, and even in the cases of many other intuitive people I have known, intuition was cultivated by a sense of permission to be more than ordinary—by a sense that as a spiritual being and a child of the Universe, I could experience and receive extraordinary guidance and support in every way. I am intuitive because I was encouraged at all times to be awake, aware, and guided by my soul. I grew up in an environment that treated intuition as *normal*. Intuition is a gift that we all deserve, that we can all experience and pass along to our own children. It is one that my husband, Patrick, and I are already passing along to our two daughters.

But what if you, as a child or as an adult and parent, were never given the gift of such an understanding of your spiritual nature or a family environment that supported this truth? Will that prevent you from being able to tap into and pass along this inner wisdom to your children today?

Not at all. That's why I have written this book. As an intuitive and a teacher of intuition for over twenty-eight years, I have made the exciting discovery that intuition, the voice of the Inner Teacher within us all, can be developed at any time, once we learn how. It is waiting for your recognition and attention and, once received, will guide and direct you as it has me. By first nurturing your own intuition, you will be able to do the same for your children.

In my years of teaching intuitive awareness to adults, and in my years as a mother of two intuitive children, I have come to believe that we can all activate an awareness of the soul and create a spiritual home atmosphere that will nurture and strengthen our most advanced perceptions. Through my own experience I have gained a working understanding of what cultivates this golden inner voice, and it is my greatest desire to share this understanding with you and all families, so that everyone everywhere will connect to the inner peace and creative direction we all have within us.

THE THREE STAGES OF NURTURING INTUITION

The most important thing I have learned about nurturing intuition in the family is that it develops in three key stages. The first stage is awakening your personal intuitive awareness. Until we become aware of our own intuition it usually lies dormant, ignored and out of reach in our own and our children's consciousness. We must first become aware that we have a sixth sense in order to develop and benefit from it. Only then can we pass on this gift to our children. Therefore the first step in nurturing intuition is to sharpen and expand our own awareness. I will discuss this in the first section.

Embracing intuition when it does show up in our lives is the second stage in developing our sixth sense. Being aware of intuition is not enough to benefit from its profound and life-changing direction. You must then decide to trust the guidance you receive from your "inner teacher," accepting its counsel as a deeply felt and welcome influence in your life and in your home. This means entering into a state of receptivity for intuitive direction at all times and being willing to embrace its wisdom when it does appear. Therefore the second section of this book will concentrate on how to accept and embrace intuition wholeheartedly in the family. It will also offer practical daily suggestions and tools to help identify and overcome obstacles to your intuition and help you recognize and honor intuitive feelings in all family members.

Asking the Universe for intuitive support is the third stage in nurturing intuition in the family. Moving into this stage of intuitive development means integrating intuition as the most important and desirable influence in making your own and your family's decisions. It also means moving past simply being aware of and receptive to intuition and into actually seeking its counsel as the primary guiding voice in your life. The third section of this book teaches you how to call upon intuition as an actual and reliable support. It includes intuitive practices and exercises that can be used comfortably by parents and children alike in order to call upon intuition to illuminate our way in life, as it is naturally meant to do.

Connecting to our intuition unites us with both our soul and the soul of the Universe, Divine Spirit. It takes away our fearful sense of isolation and inadequacy. It replaces fear with a sense of spiritual direction and safety. The world becomes friendly, nonadversarial, and welcoming. Life becomes joyful, amusing, generous, and abundant. This is the divine plan. The intuitive life is one of confidence, inner peace, and creative expression. What better gift to ourselves and our children?

Expanding Your Awareness

AWAKENING YOUR OWN INTUITION begins with training your awareness to expand and receive more information from others, from your Higher Self and from God. It is learning how to expand your consciousness and better understand how your instrument of expression—your body—receives and responds to energy. It is the art of evolving your consciousness into a highly sophisticated receiver of vibrations, thus giving you more accurate information to work with as you interact with others in this life. It is training yourself to be open and receptive to the subtle planes of energy that constitute our intuitive lives. It is living a life that communes with spirit, that sees *into* rather than looks *at* things, and that is open and responsive to the guidance of the Universe at all times. Being intuitive means being fully conscious of the spiritual nature of who you are and understanding that as a spiritual being you can expect extraordinary levels of insight at any given time, from subtle impulses to full-blown psychic experiences such as clairaudience, clairvoyance, telepathy, and even precognition.

Awakening your intuition begins with an awareness of ten basic principles. They are as follows:

1. Intuition and psychic awareness are gifts of the soul.

2. We are all souls, therefore we are all intuitive and can even become psychic.

3. Developing our intuitive natures is our spiritual birthright.

4. Intuitive feelings are messages that come from a divine source and direct us to our own divine nature and our highest creative expression.

5. Intuitive, soulful guidance benefits us all.

6. Intuition is activated by love and results in understanding.

7. An intuitive life is gentle, powerful, and always noncoercive.

8. True intuition does not flatter the ego; rather, it supports the soul's true essence.

9. An intuitive life activates our full potential.

10. Living an intuitive life yourself is the best way to pass on this important inner wisdom to your children.

* * *

Part I will focus on beginning to heighten awareness of your intuitive nature in four basic ways:

1. First we will look at your family of origin background and present-day family dynamics and suggest ways to create intuition-friendly attitudes among family members.

2. Then we will focus on intuition as the synthesis of heightened awareness, originating in your heart and then moving upward into your consciousness.

3. Next we will identify common distractions and obstacles, which prevent you from being fully aware of and receptive to intuitive guidance, and introduce techniques that will help you eliminate these tendencies.

4. Finally we will look at your home atmosphere and suggest ways to create a more sensitive and supportive environment for living an intuitive life.

Now that we know our direction, let's begin!

ONE

Awareness Begins with You

Intuition is the voice of our soul. It is an integral part of our spiritual anatomy, and its seeds lie waiting to germinate in all of us. All children will demonstrate signs of awakening intuition sooner or later—of that you can be certain. Activating these seeds of soulful awareness in your children is not the challenge; providing a framework for their fledgling intuition to thrive and become strong is. If your children notice you paying attention to your intuition, they will notice their own. If they hear you sharing your intuitive feelings, they will begin to share their experiences as well. If they notice you ignoring your intuition, they will ignore theirs. If you are comfortable with your intuition and embrace it freely and naturally as part of your spiritual makeup, then your children too will embrace their spiritual anatomy and come to depend on it as they would any other sense.

I have observed a wide variety of family attitudes about intuitive feelings, from the most dismissive ("It's only a coincidence!") to the most irrational ("It's weird") to the most suspicious ("You can't trust it") to flat-out rejection ("That's ridiculous!") and everything in between. But it is only in those families with the attitude "Intuition is the guiding voice of our souls and a natural and important part of who we are" that it really develops into the tool for inner spiritual direction that it is intended to be.

Take a moment and reflect on your family beliefs around intuition. You may recognize one of the attitudes I describe as similar to your own, or you may become clear on how your own upbringing and family perspective differed. The point is to identify and examine the roots of your own attitude and outlook regarding the guiding wisdom of your soul. This family archaeology will give you a sense of what you can build on or perhaps overcome in awakening to your intuition.

THE INTUITIVE FAMILY

In our household, guided by my intuitive mother, decisions were driven not by logic, but by instinct. It wasn't that logic was abandoned altogether—it was just that logic took a backseat to vibes. My mom's intuition surfaced spontaneously and often. And when it did, she listened to it, and so did we.

I grew up in Denver, and it was our family tradition to picnic in the mountains on Sundays. I remember one Sunday, after gathering up the basket and getting ready to head home, my mother suddenly turned to my father and said, "Let's take the scenic route instead of the main highway."

My father, who was tired, said, "Why? It will take us an hour longer." With seven kids stuffed into the back of the car, all squabbling, he could hardly be blamed for balking.

"Because my vibes say so," my mother insisted. "Humor me, please."

Sensing that my mother wasn't going to give in to reason, my father agreed and took the longer route home. Later that evening, as my parents were watching the evening news, an accident was reported. A truck carrying hazardous material had gone out of control and overturned on the main highway at just about the time we were getting ready to leave. The highway had been shut down for hours, traffic had been at a complete standstill in both directions, and people were stranded while the highway patrol attempted to clear the road. Meanwhile we had avoided the whole mess and were safe at home.

This kind of scenario was repeated so frequently in our home that following your vibes seemed to me to be the only natural way to do things. I've talked with a few other very intuitive and psychic friends and clients and asked them about the attitude toward intuition in their homes as they were growing up.

Kim, a student in one of my intuitive workshops, said that her family was very intuitively centered and that intuition was definitely expressed and even described as a physical sensation of energy.

"My mom always got a funny feeling in her belly, as she called it, whenever someone out of sight would pop into her mind—and sure enough, that person would usually telephone within hours. It happened so often that we used to laugh about it and tease her to 'answer her belly-phone' because someone was trying to reach her.

"Then there was our grandfather, her dad, who lived with us. Whenever we were faced with a decision, Papa told us to 'give it the tummy test' before we did anything."

My friend Elisa, a holistic healer, says, "In our house intuition ruled! My mother, an artist, used to say that she'd have to 'paint for inspiration' before she could find the right answer, and then she'd retreat into her studio to wait for guidance while working on a canvas. And my French grandmother, who was a fabulous cook and a real nature lover, used to tell us very clearly and with great intention that if we ever needed guidance, we should just close our eyes, breathe in deeply, and 'sniff out' the right answer. 'I can always smell trouble,' she would say seriously as she sniffed the air. 'And so can you!' "

My dearest friend and spiritual mentor, Lu Ann Glatzmaier, is an intuitive and spiritual counselor in Denver who grew up in Minnesota in a large Polish Italian family of eight kids. Like me, she had a very passionate and intuitive mother and a very grounded and pragmatic father.

Her mother's spiritual direction and strong convictions set the tone for her own intuitive and psychic insights to flourish.

"My mother was Italian, and she was one of those babies born with a veil over her face—an Italian sign for a prophet, which she very much was. Our lives were centered around her strong intuition and her keen sense of observation. Her favorite expression was, 'I'll tell you how this is going to turn out,' and then she would predict the outcome of one situation after another.

"My father was a businessman, and she called the outcome accurately on every one of his brewing deals. In spite of my father's frustration with her when she didn't agree with what he wanted to hear, he still asked for her input on things before he ever made a decision, because she was always right."

My friend Rick also grew up in a household where he was made deeply aware of his intuition and spiritual direction at a very young age—only *his* spiritual compass was set by his grounded and intuitive father.

"I remember Dad referring to his 'inner compass' as easily as he referred to the weather and suggesting to me that I had spirit guides who looked after me and protected me as well. From watching him, I learned to look inward and ask for help, taking great comfort in knowing that it was there when I needed it," Rick says. "He always summoned his intuition on matters, at times asking right out loud for guidance. Especially when we were in a jam, like when he'd get lost in the car going somewhere we'd never been before. I figured if he could ask for guidance, then so could I. And I always have."

THE NONINTUITIVE FAMILY

Nancy, one of my clients, tells of a different family atmosphere.

"Time and again I'd get these incredible feelings about people as a child and would venture occasionally to share them with my mother. Usually these 'vibes' concerned my relatives or neighbors and were often not what she wanted to hear. For example, one time I had a distinct feeling that my uncle Brian was broke even though he was considered our 'rich uncle.' I told my mom about this, but instead of listening to me, she told me to 'stop making up naughty stories about Uncle Brian.' I *knew* in my heart that my feelings were right, but I got a screwed-up notion that, right or not, such feelings were impolite. So in our house intuition was frowned upon, something that upset pleasant perceptions and made my mom uneasy even though I was proved right. It seems that my uncle had a secret gambling addiction, and a year later he went bankrupt, much to the great surprise of everyone except me."

Irene, a woman in her early sixties and a student in one of my workshops, remarked, "In my home growing up, intuition simply never existed. Ours was an intellectual household, and our focus was oriented toward academics or athletics, but never on the intuitive and sensual side of life. I don't know that I *ever* recall a conversation in our household that centered on anyone's feelings, let alone their intuitive feelings! Consequently I went through life feeling as though I were blindfolded or something. I always sensed that something was missing, but I didn't even know what it was or where to begin looking for it."

Gail recalls growing up in a home that was openly hostile to intuition. When she was young, about seven or eight years old, she remembers being quite intuitive, even psychic at times, but when she shared her feelings with her very conservative and religious parents, she would be sent to her room to "pray and drive the demons out." Of course, this left her feeling profoundly shameful and confused.

"I just couldn't get rid of those 'demons,' as my mom called them. I saw energy fields around people. I was telepathic. I could sometimes even sense events before they happened. I tried to warn everyone when I felt danger, but they didn't want to hear it.

"Once we were about to leave for my aunt's house and suddenly I had a feeling that we shouldn't go. It was as though something were trying to keep me home. I pretended that I was sick so they'd forget about the trip, but no luck. They yelled at me to stop wasting time and get in the car. I blurted out, 'I have a bad feeling. We shouldn't go!' Sure enough, I got a handful of my father's knuckles while he told me what he thought of my 'feelings.'

"We left anyway, and about half an hour later the sky blackened and the most frightening wind came barreling out of nowhere, tossing the car every which way. To our horror, we saw a tornado touching down. We all got out of the car and ran like mad toward some trees— terrified. We stayed there until the storm passed. Debris was strewn everywhere. Fortunately we were only shaken up. I knew that my feelings were a warning, but my mom and dad didn't understand. From then on I learned to hide my vibes and wanted to shut them down, which I eventually succeeded in doing."

THE DIVIDED FAMILY

No matter what your family background is regarding intuitive and psychic feelings, unfortunately the odds are that when you marry you will find yourself rooted in yet another confusing family dynamic: the divided family. In such a family, one member tends to be very intuitive and open-minded while the other leans toward a more logical, rational, and conservative point of view. Though ideally each of us incorporates both perspectives in dealing with the world, in reality we tend to be more developed and biased in one perspective or the other. Picking a partner with an opposing perspective is a natural, although usually unconscious, reaching for balance.

Problems arise when this dynamic becomes polarized, with each member of the family fixed in his or her perspective to the exclusion of any other. In this case one parent is extremely intuitive and conceptual, with a weak sense of grounding or organization around it, forcing the other parent to overcompensate by shutting out intuition altogether and becoming fixed and narrow-minded. The end result, not surprisingly, is two people at war with one another. I call this the "One's the Gas, the Other's the Brakes" syndrome, and I've been caught in it myself from time to time.

When each partner invalidates the other's perspective, a psychic tug-of-war settles in. If such tension exists in your house, it will cause problems that can push intuition out the door.

Such was the case for Eleanor, a very intuitive and devoted mother of three children. Eleanor was married to a successful structural engineer who spent a fair amount of time away from home on civic building projects. Eleanor worked hard to develop her intuition and asked me how she could instill an intuitive and soulful sense in her children.

"But," she qualified, "I have to do it in such a way that my husband, Marvin, won't find out. He thinks I'm nuts and gets annoyed when I talk to my kids about 'gut feelings' or 'vibes' or anything like it. He tells me that I'm 'not being sensible' and that I should be realistic. He's so unwilling to acknowledge anything other than the physical world that it drives me crazy! We argue constantly, which is exhausting. I just don't want my kids bullied by him the way I am."

Eleanor had a real dilemma. She wanted her children to develop their intuition but at the same time asked them to hide it from their father—quite a mixed message. Needless to say, it didn't work with the kids. Instead the two older ones shared their father's perspective, laughing at Eleanor's intuitive inclinations while ignoring their own. But the youngest child, perhaps in loyalty to Eleanor, tuned in to his intuition and openly expressed his feelings and vibes, to the annoyance of his dad and siblings. Everyone, believing themselves to be right, discounted the opposing points of view, setting off spontaneous arguments and snide remarks. It was unpleasant, to be sure.

I told Eleanor that my spiritual and psychic teachers had trained me to understand that intuition complements logic; it does not compete with or negate it. I suggested to Eleanor that she stop disregarding Marvin's opinion and listen to it instead. After all, he had achieved quite a lot in his profession that deserved respect, not to mention the fact that he was also a reliable marriage partner and a strong and committed father to his children. He couldn't be as totally unaware as she believed and still be as successful as he had. He simply had a different perspective from her own on things, one that reflected both his strengths *and* blind spots.

"Move toward balance, Eleanor," I suggested. "Imagine your family as a tree. See you and your youngest son as the leaves and branches of the tree, expansive, intuitive, reaching outward toward the unknown, while envisioning Marvin and your older kids as the roots and trunk, grounded, protective, and rooted in the familiar. In spite of the discomfort this creates, you *need* each other. When you negate each other's perspectives, you block your own ability to see the larger picture. Such intolerance for another perspective will actually work against your own intuition in the long run. You need to respect each other's vantage points in order to create stability and encourage growth.

"Open your mind and be willing to see the whole picture. One of the fundamentals of intuition is listening and learning all that you can about a situation, especially things you may have overlooked or don't understand, before drawing your conclusions."

Eleanor agreed to try this. She began by acknowledging and respecting her husband's opinion, even though at times it was hard not to disagree or interrupt. She honestly opened her mind, and to her surprise, on occasion, Marvin even made sense.

At first Marvin was shocked at Eleanor's new attitude; then he began acting like a know-it-all, as if to say to her, "I'm glad you've come back to earth." But after a month or so he actually approached Eleanor and asked for her vibes on whether or not he should commit to a new building project located in another town. She couldn't believe it! She wanted to laugh out loud at his reversal, but she restrained herself. After all those years of invalidating her intuition, he was actually seeking it now. Having been heard himself, he was now willing to listen to her. And to Eleanor's great surprise, after listening to her point of view, he actually followed her advice.

Eleanor's outcome was a successful shift from family polarity to one of balance. Eventually her kids began subtly to reflect the shift in attitude as well. Her young son moved toward more objectivity, asking questions of his father more often, while the two older kids began asking Eleanor for guidance in the name of "good fun" more often than ever before.

Polarity in a family causes frustration and unnecessary competition. Everyone involved feels invalidated. And it's foolish as well, because a highly developed intuitive sense cannot be effective unless our faculties of reason are also brought into play. Even the greatest insights are useless unless they can be integrated into our lives through reason. Intuition is not irrational, nor does it require you to invalidate or ignore reason or tune out your other five senses.

Quite the contrary. Intuition works best when a person is well informed by the other senses. In fact, one of the definitions of intuition is "to pay attention to." This is because paying attention is central to heightened awareness. God did not set up our spiritual anatomy to compete with our physical anatomy. The first five senses are not intended to negate intuition; they are intended to complement and support it.

Eleanor and Marvin, being positioned at opposite ends of the intuition spectrum, naturally attracted each other as they strove unconsciously for balance, as you may have done in your own family. In their case, as they failed to recognize their complementary natures, a battle ensued, one that drew in the children as well. But when they began to see each other's perspectives as the missing piece in their own biased point of view, appreciation and resolution followed. Intuition was finally invited into their family, where it took up welcome residence alongside reason. Understanding and creating harmonious family dynamics is key to bringing intuition home. As long as polarized viewpoints exist, intuition will not be able to assume its proper place comfortably in either you or your household. As long as this sort of opposition is present, whether between spouses or between parents and children, you and your family will no doubt be too caught up in the struggle to even notice intuition.

REALITY CHECK

Take the following intuition awareness quiz to see where you are in relationship to your intuition today and whether or not you or your family members are interfering with each other's intuitive feelings:

	RARELY	SOMETIMES	OFTEN
I am aware of how I feel around certain people.	___	___	___
I trust my first impressions about people and situations.	___	___	___

I easily notice my intuitive feelings. _____ _____ _____

I talk openly and comfortably about intuition
at home. _____ _____ _____

I follow my instincts no matter what my family
members feel. _____ _____ _____

My family members' attitudes affect me a lot
when it comes to trusting my intuition. _____ _____ _____

I can change my mind and decisions easily if I
get a gut feeling to do so, even if it will upset
someone in the family. _____ _____ _____

I can feel when my children and family are in
trouble. _____ _____ _____

I have lots of coincidences in my life, especially
concerning my family. _____ _____ _____

My family and my children respect my intuition,
and I listen to and respect theirs. _____ _____ _____

I follow my gut even if my family advises me in
another way. _____ _____ _____

I can stand up to opposing energy, for either my
children or myself. _____ _____ _____

I look to my intuition when making decisions and
encourage my kids to do the same. _____ _____ _____

I make no attempt to hide my intuitive feelings,
especially at home or with those close to me. _____ _____ _____

When you have completed the quiz, go back and look at your answers. Give yourself:

1 point for each "Rarely"
2 points for each "Sometimes"
3 points for each "Often"

If your score was 1–15:
Apparently you were not taught to listen to or value your intuition as a child, so you hesitate to do so today. Perhaps you have attracted a partner who does value intuition, although this may make you nervous. Don't worry—your intuition is simply lying dormant, and you will relax and embrace intuition more comfortably as you begin to use the tools in the following chapters.

If your score was 16–30:
You were probably made aware of intuition when you were young but most likely lived in an ambivalent or opposing atmosphere surrounding it. Perhaps you are in a polarized dynamic with your partner, flip-flopping day by day from confidence to questioning. Be encouraged. Simply being aware of intuition goes a long way toward strengthening your confidence in your own vibes while avoiding conflicts with your partner. You, your partner, and your children will soon delight in its wonderful benefits.

If your score was 31–45:
You undoubtedly were one of those people gifted with a nurturing atmosphere toward intuition and probably are well on your way to passing on this gift to your children. Celebrate this blessing as you move directly into expanding even more in sharing your inner wisdom and vision with your family.

RESTORING HARMONY
No matter what the beliefs were in your family of origin, or whether or not you find yourself in a polarized situation in your family today, you

can still develop your own intuition as well as foster intuition in your children by restoring harmony. All it takes is a willingness on your part to be gentle and open-minded with your family and yourself to end the problem and move everyone closer to experiencing intuition's healing benefits firsthand.

The best way to do this is to take a holistic approach toward introducing intuition, which means appreciating everyone's points of view. If you have the right attitude, there are several ways to dismantle polarity and confusion and shift the atmosphere to a more welcoming one.

The first way is to ask yourself if a polarized or negative perspective is set up within you.

* Are you overly analytical and physically focused?
* Are you cynical or suspicious of the validity of intuition?
* Do you disallow or ignore the unseen, hidden factors in life?

If so, you may be a died-in-the-wool pragmatist or carry over some past negative attitudes from your family of origin. If you believe this is the case, practice noticing new things and looking past appearances for the nuances and more subtle aspects of life.

* Try to notice something new about each member of your family.
* Invite them to do the same for you.
* See how many new things you can notice that you haven't ever noticed before.

Realize that your intuition is like an unexercised muscle and that it needs a workout to remain sharp and receptive.

* Ask yourself whether you are excessively controlling and may actually avoid situations and people because you may not be able to control them.

Introducing intuition into your home definitely invites new and unforeseen aspects into your life, and listening to it requires that you loosen your control over things a bit. Practice this in little, nonthreatening ways every day. For instance:

* Go on a spontaneous outing to someplace new.
* Try taking a new route to work, and enjoy the scenery.
* Practice listening to someone you would otherwise ignore or tune out.

Another way to open your mind and become more intuitive is to become aware of the difference between what is real and what is actually a projection of your worries and fears. Many people confuse their greatest worries and darkest fears for reality, and in the name of logic, they irrationally draw all kinds of narrow-minded, inaccurate, and suspicious conclusions about people or situations before they give themselves a chance to discover what they are really about. This tendency eliminates all kinds of synchronistic and creative possibilities. To make sure that you don't fall into this trap, actively practice staying focused on what you know to be real, and be open to discovering what is true and genuine in all situations. Keep from letting a defensive or reactive mind-set distort reality or confuse your judgment and cut you off from your intuitive feelings and their possible benefits.

JOIN IN LAUGHTER AND PLAY

Another way to overcome a polarized or a negative attitude toward intuition is to approach it in a lighthearted, playful way, one that invites all members of the family to join in.

I had a client named Robert who was very intuitive and tried to use his intuition as much as possible in his field as a stockbroker. Predicting market trends was a favorite game of his and one he frequently encouraged his eight- and ten-year-old children to join him in playing. Of course, having been thoroughly trained in market analysis, he employed many other factors as well in his investment decisions. But, he confessed, intuition was definitely his favorite. Not only did he find his intuition to be effective in anticipating market shifts, he discovered that his kids were even more accurate in their intuitive determinations than he was. What frustrated Robert no end was the fact that his wife, Ruth, completely opposed their intuitive musings and insisted that they stop. She interrupted him when he talked about using his intuition in his work and got very annoyed with him when he encouraged the kids to give him their hunches on his investment decisions, saying, "This is no better than gambling, Robert. It's reckless and irresponsible, not only with our money, but with other people's money as well!" It didn't matter to her that no harm was done. It was threatening to her sense of how things worked, and she didn't like it.

Robert, however, didn't feel as though he were being reckless at all, and, in fact, he and the kids were having a great time outsmarting the market experts with their vibes. Not only did he not lose money, together he and the kids were actually profiting by using the "vibe method," as they humorously called it.

The problem for Robert and his boys was that they never really invited Ruth to join in on the fun. Theirs was a polarity of practicality (Ruth's position) and play (Robert's position) in their relationships with the kids.

"Do you ever ask Ruth about her vibes or her feelings on the markets?" I asked Robert.

"Good grief, no!" he answered emphatically. "I don't think she'd even know what a vibe is, she's so concrete."

"That's the problem right there, Robert. You're cutting her off from her intuition."

"Me? How?"

"Because," I said, "you're so convinced that what you *know* of her is all there is to know. In your certainty that she is fixed, you are actually reinforcing her fixed tendencies and preventing her from exploring or engaging any other side of herself. You and the kids are boxing her in."

"Hmmm. I can see what you mean," he said thoughtfully. "I don't want to do that!"

"My teacher Dr. Tully said one of the best ways to tap intuition and bring it out in others is to never assume you know someone or something completely," I continued. "Always leave room for surprise."

"Let me think about that," Robert said.

The next time I saw Robert he had quite a different picture to paint about his wife and the family vibe sessions. "I took your advice and encouraged the kids to join me in asking Ruth what her vibes were on things," he said. "At first she ignored us, but we didn't give up. We teased her, prodded her, and actually started to have fun with her. Every time she'd say, 'I bet . . .' we'd ask her, 'Is that a vibe?'

"Finally she started easing up a little and even offered us a tip or two of her own, on the condition that I not actually put money on it! That is, of course, until she had a few successful calls. That changed everything. We were all so surprised to discover her intuitive side, most of all her. She began paying more and more attention to her intuitive feelings. Though she is still conservative, she is now more open and is participating in the fun. We haven't gotten rich on our intuition, but we are ahead of the game. And the best part is, we no longer isolate our intuition to money matters. With Ruth's influence, we are now using our intuition on the kids' schoolwork, grocery shopping, and even where to vacation as a family this summer. In other words, in the things she's interested in and has a feel for. Our entire family dynamic has changed completely, and we have all learned something new."

DON'T BE AN INTUITIVE SNOB

Though many people tend to err on the side of being intuitively shut down, others go overboard in the other direction and feel their intuition is the *only* thing worth considering. They believe their intuition precludes the need to listen to any other input or consider anyone else's feelings. Usually such intuitive enthusiasts act smug and superior, while often feeling unappreciated by their intimate others.

If you are such an intuitive type and you feel disrespected, misunderstood, or invalidated by your partner or other family member, ask yourself if you aren't doing the same to them.

* Do you act like a spiritual know-it-all, discounting others as disconnected?

* Do you secretly think you are more evolved, an enlightened being among "mere mortals"?
* Do you fail to appreciate the grounding given to you by your more practical intimates?
* Do you use your intuition as a way to tune others out or to invalidate their opinions?

I've noticed that some budding intuitives quickly adopt an attitude of superiority around those who remain disconnected from their intuition, an attitude that is ironically felt intuitively by those very same others and resented. Ask yourself if in using your intuition you are being irresponsible about staying grounded and respectful of the physical plane.

For example, my husband and I used to have a running battle about my refusal to lock our doors. I intuitively felt that we were safe, but he finally made a very good point that got through to me. "Trust the Universe, Sonia," Patrick said, "but don't tempt it!"

He was right. I now lock the doors.

Another suggestion is to be considerate when asking your family members to respect your intuition. Intuition shows up spontaneously and often requires quick, decisive responses, even sudden and abrupt changes of course. This sort of spontaneity can upset some people and arouse their fears. You may collide head-on with the fears of other family members if you aren't careful. I've found that simply being sensitive to the temperaments of others will often clear the way for intuition to enter. When my intuition suggests sudden change, I explain to my family that my inner direction is giving me guidance that might "rock the boat" and that I need their cooperation. Simply being asked rather than told to give their cooperation is usually all they need to agree to accept my intuition and do as I ask.

Asking that your intuition be respected rather than imposing it on the family fosters goodwill and will often shift a negative family member into a more positive and receptive frame of mind. It prevents you from appearing like an insensitive know-it-all and keeps respect operating in both directions. One simple way to do this is to ask the family, as my mother did, to "humor me" if necessary.

WHEN ALL ELSE FAILS

In spite of the techniques I've mentioned, there will always be some people who are stuck in their points of view and stubbornly refuse to shift into soulful awareness. They may be close-minded spouses, old-fashioned parents, or even cynical children. No matter how good your intentions are in bringing intuition and soulful awareness into your home, you may encounter someone who will stubbornly resist.

I have a client named Polly who is a massage therapist and the mother of two teenagers, ages seventeen and nineteen. She is married to a lawyer. Through her studies and her body work Polly has really awakened her intuition and is now sharing this awareness with her kids, who in turn are tapping into their own. They are having a great adventure and are benefiting from it enormously. But as hard as they try to persuade him, Polly's husband, Peter, is still completely turned off by the whole world of "vibes" and absolutely refuses to join in, to shift out of polarity or into play. He is disgusted with all of them and says so. Polly's husband is stuck on the old messages he received from his superstitious mother and his overly analytical father, messages that said the intuitive world was not a spiritual one or a valid one. Until he gains an understanding to the contrary, he will most likely maintain his suspicious and contemptuous point of view.

I suggested to Polly that now is her opportunity to move into the position of teacher with him, just as she is doing for her children. The best way to do this would be to assume a neutral attitude and not let his negative projections distract her from her positive experience. I suggested that she treat him with quiet acceptance, recognizing that he is ill informed and afraid and that his fear is not something she needs to wrestle with. I encouraged her to stay on course, continue to openly share her feelings with her children, to freely discuss the positive benefits the three of them are experiencing, and to politely ignore her husband's potshots. "Eventually he'll tire of throwing them, especially if he doesn't get a reaction," I told her.

I had one more suggestion for Polly. "Try introducing a more acceptable language into your conversations about intuition. It could very well be that the words you use, like 'spirit,' 'vibes,' and so forth, trigger some reaction in him. Try using more commonplace words, like 'I'll bet' or 'gut feeling,' 'I have a hunch' or 'It seems to me.' You may get a less emotional reaction.

"And above all, be loving toward him. After all, one of the functions of intuition is to help you see the true nature of things even when he can't. The truth is that even he is a spiritual being, worthy of love and acceptance. Don't set yourself up for failure by demanding that he accept something he is not quite able to yet. After all, he married you, didn't he? He's the father of your intuitive children. Some part of his nature is willing to grow in understanding or he wouldn't be with you three. Just be patient with him."

In Polly's case the suggestions worked. She stopped trying to convince her husband to open up. She changed her vocabulary and ignored his rude remarks. She called me one day to report that in fact he had mellowed out and eventually lost interest in making negative remarks. "It's as though we've silently agreed to tolerate one another. Now when the kids and I tell each other about our intuitive experiences, he doesn't leave the room the way he used to. Instead he picks up the paper and pretends to read, but we all know he's really listening, and it makes us smile."

When you're around people who are stuck, as Peter was, avoid trying to change or reform their attitude—or, worse yet, gang up on them. It will only further distance them from being receptive, and it will make you look and feel controlling. Intuitive life is never to be lived as a campaign for reform. Let your own positive and peaceful way of life, with its synchronicities, "ah-ha!" moments, and delightful gifts from the Universe, speak for you. A family is a very tight unit. Even the most narrow-minded will take note of such changes and improvements. If you don't invalidate their point of view, they are more likely to accept yours.

* * *

Reflection FAMILY ARCHAEOLOGY

Take a moment and reflect on your own family background regarding intuition.

1. What was your mother's attitude toward intuitive feelings?

_____

_____

_____

2. Did she freely express her feelings, or did she hide them?

_____

_____

_____

3. If she did express her vibes, what value did she place on them? (For example, did she listen to her own intuition, or did she dismiss it?)

_____

_____

_____

4. Was she superstitious about her intuitive feelings? How?

_____

_____

_____

5. Did she follow her intuition, or did she defer her feelings to your father or some other person?

_____

_____

_____

6. Was she confident or insecure? How?

_____

_____

_____

7. Can you talk about intuition with your mother today?

_____

_____

_____

8. How do you feel about this?

_____

_____

_____

9. What was your father's attitude toward intuition?

_____

_____

_____

10. Was he intuitive? Did he ever express his vibes?

_____

_____

_____

11. Did he allow or encourage you to be intuitive?

_____

_____

_____

12. How did your father respond to your mother's or your intuitive feelings?

_____

_____

_____

13. How do you feel about this today?

_____

_____

_____

14. Can you talk about intuition with your father?

_____

_____

_____

Tools FOR INVITING INTUITION INTO YOUR HOME

* Approach intuition with a loving, playful attitude. Keep your ego out of it.
* Discover and discuss with your family intuitive ancestors.
* Be respectful and open-minded toward all family members' opinions toward intuition, even those with closed minds.
* Avoid drama when sharing your vibes with the family. Intuition is natural, so don't overreact.

* Be tolerant and good-humored if a family member behaves in a skeptical way toward intuition.
* Avoid all "campaigns of reform."
* Encourage family members to check in with their intuitive feelings when making decisions.
* Remain aware that intuition is latent in all of us, even if others seem disbelieving or unaware.
* Avoid being a know-it-all or having a superior attitude when it comes to your instincts!
* Be open to new dimensions and insights, however subtle, from all family members.
* No matter what your history is, know that you can awaken these seeds of intuition in all family members today, through awareness, acceptance, and action.

TWO

Being Present

So many people have the false notion that intuition is tuning out the real world. Nothing could be further from the truth. Strange as it may seem, in order to become aware of the voice of your soul and tune in to your intuition, it is first necessary to be fully conscious of what is here and now. My spiritual teacher Dr. Tully taught me that the key to developing intuition is to pay keen attention to the world around us today. He told me that people are confused when they think intuition is tuning in to some otherworldly frequency. "True intuition," he explained, "is the consequence of clear and accurate observations of the here and now. It is these accurate observations, once turned over to the subconscious mind, that lead to the most advanced insights." In other words, you need to be fully aware and present in the moment to even notice your intuition.

So many of us today are so overbooked, juggling too many things at one time, constantly playing "catch-up," and racing around like crazy, that we often end up diminishing our awareness to nothing more than a whirling gray fog of confusion. We miss the most obvious of situations, never mind being able to tune in to the more subtle, intuitive aspects of things.

One day years ago, when my children were only one and two years old, I sat exhausted on the front porch after a long day at work and watched the girls playing in front of the house while Patrick watered the lawn. After a few minutes a pleasant-looking woman walked up to Patrick, and the two of them chatted briefly. Then she smiled at me and continued down the street.

"Who's that, Patrick?" I asked.

Patrick looked at me in disbelief. "Sonia, that's our neighbor, who's been living next door for the past six months." He shook his head in wonder that I didn't know her.

"You're kidding," I answered. "I've never seen her before."

"Yes, you have!" Patrick insisted. "You've seen her hundreds of times. You've just never paid *attention* to her before!"

Boy, did I ever feel like a fool. Patrick was right. Since the birth of Sabrina, my life had speeded up so much that it had become a blur. I spent my days trying to manage so much—the two girls both in diapers; rehabbing our two-unit building with Patrick while he worked two jobs; keeping up on my one-on-one work with clients; and giving workshops. All of this was crammed into a very short twenty-four-hour day, and I was so overwhelmed with so much activity that there were days I couldn't even remember what I had done, let alone notice my family. Now, staring at a neighbor as if she were a complete stranger, I realized that in my effort to do it all I had spiraled right out of my own body and off the planet Earth. I was so "otherly" focused that I had lost the ability to see the nose in front of my face. My awareness had truly shriveled up.

Though Patrick and I laughed about it at the time, that experience was a real wake-up call for me. "Where was I? Where have I been? Where has my awareness been lately?" I asked myself. As I reflected on the previous year I could hardly bring any of it into focus. Nothing stood out. As I watched my girls carefully scrutinizing the ants on the sidewalk, I realized that in all my hurried doings I hadn't *really* been present in my life. Not to them. Not to anything.

I watched my daughters gleefully examining a fallen leaf. First Sonia eyeballed it very closely, and then she handed it to Sabrina, who promptly popped it into her mouth. It felt good to be back in the moment, leaving my mental rat race behind. I took in a long, deep breath, savoring the air as it filled my lungs and energized me. As I exhaled and sat in that quiet moment before the next breath, my awareness exploded into a symphony of acute sensuality. I began to notice things I hadn't noticed before. Colors became brighter. Sounds became crisper. My children were no longer mental extensions of me, but returned to being the unique and precious beings that they were. It was as if someone had just tuned my mental TV channel from fuzzy black and white to sharp, brilliant color.

Slowly, even luxuriously, I took another breath. Sonia tottered toward me, screaming, "Mommy, a ladybug!" Sabrina spat out her leaf and followed her sister. Sonia held up her baby hand to me, and right in the middle of it was a bright orange-red ladybug with black dots. The minute I looked at it, it flew away.

In that moment I decided that I absolutely had to *slow down*! I had to stop racing around in my mind, trying frantically to cover all the bases. I had to stop scheduling every minute of my day down to the nanosecond, leaving me no time to be aware of anything. I had to back off from my nose-to-the-grindstone, hyperdrive tempo of trying to keep it all together and simply breathe and trust that my slowing down would not compromise a thing. In fact, it was essential if I wanted to be a good mother and, more important, to arm my children with such necessary life tools as intuition and clear vision. I myself had to stop the insane and unconscious pace of do it all that had removed my awareness from planet Earth.

"So this is what Dr. Tully meant when he said intuition arises out of a keen sense of the here and now," I thought as I watched Sabrina digging in the dirt and Sonia very carefully sticking her toes into the water sprinkler. They are noticing everything in this moment by having a *very direct* experience with the world around them—right now! This is where intuition is born. This is the first lesson in awareness.

STAY IN THE MOMENT

Noticing and experiencing our surroundings requires an acute presence of mind. Children are born with this presence. They watch everything deeply, closely, and carefully. They don't miss a thing. But what do *we* notice as rushed, preoccupied, overextended parents? If your life is the way mine was at the time, not much. And if we don't notice the world, how well informed can we be about it? The less informed we are about circumstances, the less likely we are to draw the right conclusions and make the best decisions for ourselves and for our children. In order to foster intuition, you must sharpen your awareness and accurately inform yourself about the nature of things around you, and that requires allowing enough *time* to do so.

I am very sympathetic to parents who have heavy schedules, because life as a parent involves so much planning. I know it is hard to stay in the moment. But there are things you can do to slow down and be present with children, even while you struggle to keep up with life's demands. The first thing you can do is practice meditating.

Meditation

Meditation is the most effective way to sharpen your awareness because it clears away the mental noise and distractions that prevent you from noticing what is important here and now. Meditation helps you become more relaxed, balanced, and present to the moment. If you've never meditated, don't worry. It's not difficult. It is quite simply the art of relaxing your body, resting your emotions, and quieting your mind for fifteen minutes a day. There are no tricks to meditation, but there are techniques that make it easier.

> Meditation begins with focusing on your breath.
> Start by taking in a deep breath right now and
> notice how much your awareness expands when
> you simply do this. Take a few more deep, cleansing

breaths, and then allow your breath to settle into an easy, rhythmic pattern.

Next, gently close your eyes. Notice the difference simply closing your eyes makes in your level of relaxation. With your eyes closed, continue to breathe in to the count of four, hold it to the count of four, and then exhale to the count of four. If thoughts arise during this exercise, simply observe them and then go back to your breath. Don't fight or struggle with each new thought. Observe it as though it is one of a string of train cars moving through the night, entering into and then drifting out of your consciousness.

Continue breathing and relaxing for fifteen minutes, then gently open your eyes and go about your day.

That's it! You've just meditated. Fifteen minutes a day of meditation is all that is necessary to clear your mind, heighten your awareness, and bring you fully into the moment.

To deepen your meditation experience, you may want to say a few gentle, repetitive, calming phrases to yourself while breathing, such as, "I am . . ." on the inhale and ". . . at peace" on the exhale. You may even want to play some ambient or classical music such as Vivaldi or Pachelbel quietly in the background while meditating to further assist you in achieving a quiet inner state.

The best way to assure successful deep meditation is to be consistent. It is by far more effective to meditate every day at the same time for fifteen minutes than randomly once a week for an hour. A busy parent's schedule does make it tricky to find the time to meditate consistently, so you will have to select a time that works best for you. I personally prefer meditating in the morning upon waking and before getting out of bed. I simply prop myself sitting up on my pillow and begin. One of my clients, Louise, a part-time working mother of twin boys, found that she meditates best just after putting the boys down for their afternoon nap. Joan, another working mother of teenage girls, meditates on her lunch hour, because she finds there is just never any time at home.

"I AM CALM"

Another presence-enhancing technique that will help you come back to the moment and raise your awareness is one my husband, Patrick, who teaches meditation, taught me years ago. When you are under stress, overwhelmed, rushed, or preoccupied, simply touch your thumb and forefinger together and say quietly to yourself, "I am . . ." on the inhale, and ". . . calm" on the exhale. Allow the word "calm" to reverberate throughout your entire body. The act of touching thumb to forefinger is a physical reminder to come back to the moment, and the words "I am calm" wash away the stress.

SIMPLIFY AND SLOW DOWN

Another way to enhance your awareness and become more present in the moment is to simplify your commitments and allow yourself more time to relax. I have discovered that part of the reason some of us are so unaware and distracted is that we are juggling too many balls at once, and in trying to keep up with all our obligations, we never have a moment to relax.

For example, I once had a client named Josephine who ran her own dressmaking business while parenting three boys, ages seven, nine, and thirteen. She also ran the Parent-Teacher Association, taught yoga classes twice a week, belonged to a book club, and helped her realtor husband part-time as a secretary—all in addition to taking her kids to soccer games, basketball tournaments, and piano lessons. She never went anywhere without her portable phone, her portfolio, a beeper, and a "to do" list from here to the end of the millennium.

Initially Josephine prided herself on her ability to manage so much, but eventually signs of stress appeared. Finally she came to see me for an appointment because she was having memory lapses, forgetting appointments, losing patience, spacing out, and generally confusing her commitments at an ever-increasing rate. It was frightening her, not to mention annoying her clients and family.

"Sonia, do you think I'm all right?" she asked me anxiously. "I'm so forgetful and so temperamental that I'm out of control. I have no patience with the boys. I yell at them all the time, and I can hardly stand to be with them because they're so loud and rambunctious. I'm not myself at all."

It didn't take a great effort on my part to see how absolutely over-committed Josephine was and that this was her sole problem. Her memory lapses and confusion were her mind's way of getting rid of the overload. In her zealousness to "do it all" she was in fact accomplishing less than she thought. Driven by her ambitious desire to achieve everything, she was cheating herself out of the ability to experience anything fully.

"Josephine, slow down," I suggested. "Cut back. Prioritize and delegate when you can, and let some things go! You're doing way too much, and at such a breakneck pace that it eliminates your ability to really be present at all. You're not enjoying your family or your life, and for all your effort you have only succeeded in becoming miserable and exhausted. When was the last time you had a casual conversation with one of your sons? Or played a game with them? Or read a book together? Or simply hung out with them?"

"I can't remember." She sighed. "I'm too busy working, or I'm too impatient when I think of all I have to do."

Josephine needed a change, badly. I advised her to take an objective look at her schedule, to which she agreed. In doing so, she noticed that she had packed her schedule so tightly that she had forgotten to schedule time to just *be*.

Once Josephine saw the problem she decided to make a few changes. She let go of her secretarial work, and she scheduled her own commitments on a more realistic timetable. She also hired a teenager to work a few hours a week in her office, and she resigned from the PTA position. She chose to create time simply to relax, something she'd never done before. Once she had some breathing room, she began to connect better with her husband and even became more inspired in her dress designs. The best part, however, was the deepening connection she began to feel with her sons.

In Josephine's case, cutting way back and slowing way down was the shift she needed to get out of her head and reconnect to her heart, her family, and her life.

BE INTERESTED

I truly believe one of the bedrocks of developing intuition and higher perception in children is the presence of interested and caring eyes. In the lives of a number of great creative and intuitive people, there was a very interested and caring person. Steven Spielberg, for example, had a mother who was very interested in his passions. She helped him make his first movies, even taking him out of school at times to finish a project. Long before Jane Goodall became a famous primate anthropologist, it was her mother who first moved with her to Africa to study chimpanzees. Jane was only twenty, and no one else would hear of a woman doing such a thing.

Many of my intuitive friends have had highly present and interested parents when they were young. My mentor Lu Ann, a gifted intuitive and spiritual scholar, had a mother who readily shared Lu's passion for philosophical query and a father who was more than happy to engage in deep discussions with her. My friend Ron, a musician and composer, had a very available father who bought him his first guitar and listened enthusiastically to every one of his original compositions from third grade to the present.

In my own life, my mother was very present and interested in being with us. She laughed, joked, danced, and talked with us for hours. We looked forward to sharing our day with her after school. She truly wanted to know how it went. Even the neighborhood kids came over to our house to talk with my mom. She especially shared a passion for the intuitive world with me. One of our favorite pastimes was sharing vibes and talking about spirit, and to this day I am devoted to intuitive work.

Be creative in finding ways to be more present to your children. If your life is jam-packed with obligations, get out your appointment book and commit a time to be with them before you commit yourself to everyone else. Take a few moments to talk with them before you fall exhausted into bed. Let them know that their world is worth your time and attention. Make it one of your top priorities to have the energy and presence of mind to share their experiences and interests with them before they go to sleep.

I know that many parents today were raised with a work ethic that says, "You can't relax or play until your work is done." In raising a family today, however, we know that our "work" is never done and that we must carve out time for relaxation and play. If we put off the pleasures of sharing creative time with our children until we have finished our work, we risk missing everything, a loss for both ourselves and our children that can never be recovered.

You don't need large amounts of time to touch base with your kids and share their world. Five minutes of quality presence is worth hours of preoccupied effort. Take the time, for your own spiritual well-being, for your own intuitive peace of mind, to actually get to know and enjoy and play with these light beings called your kids.

PRESENCE LENDS POWER

If you don't think such presence and awareness makes a difference in helping your children tap in to their inner strength and resources, let me tell you a story about Sonia.

This past summer Patrick rented a country farmhouse high on top of a ridge for our annual vacation. Several days after we arrived, Patrick rented a couple of old rickety bicycles to tool around on.

Arriving at the farmhouse with them, Sonia, aged nine, not surprisingly wanted to ride one. Unsure it would be safe because the road was so steep, I asked Patrick. "I think it'll be fine," he reassured me. "I'll go with her, and we'll only ride to the bottom of the hill."

So amid my cautious warnings they strapped on helmets, lowered Sonia's bicycle seat, and were off.

I had arranged to pick them up in the car in thirty minutes, and eventually it was time to meet them. I drove to the bottom of the hill just in time to see Sonia pedaling awkwardly behind Patrick, obviously having the time of her life. Happy to see she had managed so well, and turning to face the three-mile vertical climb back to the top, I said, "Good job, Sonia! Now, let's put the bike in the car and I'll drive you back."

"But Mom," she protested, "I don't want to *drive* up! I'd rather ride."

"Sonia, it's a three-mile rise!" I protested. "It's very hard even for an expert biker like your dad. You can't possibly make it!"

"You don't know," she said. "I want to try!"

She had a point. I didn't *think* that she could ride up the hill, but in fact I didn't know she couldn't do it.

"Let me ride, please!" she persisted.

Patrick and I exchanged glances, and he shrugged as if to say, "It's up to you."

"Okay, Sonia, I'll tell you what. Ride as far as you can and I'll drive the car behind you. When you feel you can't go any farther, pull over and I'll drive you the rest of the way."

"Great!" she yelled, already heading up the incline.

I followed closely behind as she pedaled steadily after her father, sandwiched protectively between us. As I watched her ride, my eyes grew wide in disbelief. She stayed behind Patrick, not slowing for even a moment.

They crested the first hill and began climbing the second without hesitation. Soon they arrived at the second crest and began inching slowly up the third. I had expected this of Patrick, who had biked for years, but I was amazed at how Sonia, struggling even to reach the pedals, kept up at his pace.

Finally they crested the last hill and coasted victoriously into the farmhouse yard. Much to my amazement, Sonia had done it! She had pedaled up a three-mile vertical rise without missing a beat!

She ripped off her helmet and ran joyously toward me. "Wow! Mom, I did it! Surprised?"

"You bet I am!" I exclaimed. "How on earth did you find the strength?"

Beaming with pride, she answered, "Easy. I imagined that Daddy pulled me and you pushed me, and I just rode along in the middle!"

One of the most profound things you as a parent can do to awaken your children's desire to reach for their own natural potential is to give them your full awareness and attention. This doesn't mean hovering over them, projecting your every fear, and being a control freak. Nor does it mean abandoning your own path. It simply means being conscious enough of them as individuals and giving them enough of your interested presence to help them want to discover for themselves who they are and what great things they can achieve.

PRESENCE PROVIDES PROTECTION

The importance of being consciously present and really being aware of your children cannot be overemphasized. I once worked with a detective, J. J. Bittenbinder, who had a TV show called *Tough Target*. We both emphasized how awareness and paying attention are key to personal safety.

I take that a step further. I believe that criminals are in their own way very intuitive, because as predators they "sniff out" their victims by noticing who is not paying attention and who is vulnerable. If you are preoccupied, relentlessly in a hurry, and rarely if ever truly aware of your children, they will emote an aura of vulnerability because of it.

I discovered this as a child of twelve with my two best girlfriends, Sue and Darlene. Both Darlene's mom and my mom were very aware, present parents, always checking on us and making us report in with them every so often when we played outside. Sue often complained bitterly about our restrictions. They cramped her style. Her own single mother worked at a dry cleaners all day and, as she proudly put it, "lets me do whatever I want."

One day the three of us were hanging out in front of my house when a car pulled up and a man of about forty leaned out of the window and beckoned our way.

"Hey, you!" he said, pointing to Sue. "Come here a minute. I'd like to talk to you."

Sue walked over, and the man asked her if she wanted to be a model. He handed her a business card and told her that he was an agent for a modeling agency looking for new talent. He said she was prettier than we were and that he wanted to hire her to work for his agency. Needless to say, Sue was incredibly flattered.

"I'd love to model," she answered breathlessly, "but first I have to ask my mother."

Then she ran over to us and very excitedly said, "I have to go, you guys. That man is from a modeling agency, and he wants to hire me! I can't believe it! I'll see you later. I'm going to call my mom and tell her the great news." Then she was off, racing toward home before we had time to ask a single question. We watched as the man in the car followed her home, feeling jealous and left out. We waited patiently for her to return and give us all the details, but after a while, when she didn't return, Darlene and I got nervous, and I told my mother what happened. At first she called Sue's house, but when she didn't get an answer, she called Sue's mother at work. Her mother was horrified when she had heard that Sue had taken off with a strange man in a car following behind her and immediately called the police. A search began, although Sue was nowhere to be found. We were all worried sick, especially Darlene and me, thinking how lucky we were that he didn't get to one of us. Later that evening Sue was found, naked and disoriented, wandering in the mountains.

Apparently the guy convinced her to get into his car and, once he had her, drove her to the mountains, where he forced her to undress and photographed her in the nude. Then he molested her and left her there. Luckily that was all. The man was never caught.

Knowing more now than I did then, I can understand why he didn't beckon to Darlene or me. I'm sure he sensed the difference in the parental presence surrounding us. As Darlene said, "I wouldn't have even asked my mom. I know what the answer would be!" It was as though the man had known intuitively which of us was the most vulnerable, the easiest to prey upon.

THE FAMILY DINNER

Being present need not be complicated and difficult. One of the simplest ways to be present for your children is to recapture the tradition of the family dinner. It is remarkable to me how many families in these times have thrown that tradition to the winds. Some people have completely forgotten the ritual of togetherness and spiritual bonding that can occur at the family table. They erroneously believe that meals are only about physical sustenance, so any drive-through window will do. The prevailing attitude is "Everyone for himself."

Family dinner offers an opportunity to share in each other's presence, noticing and enjoying each other's experiences, challenges, and contributions. It can be a time of genuine connection, a time where you and your kids experience the pleasure of being in each other's company, a time to share what's going on in your lives. It should not be a time to discuss your differences and never a place to argue. In my family, dinner was when we shared stories, told jokes, and discovered what each person was up to. The family dinner was central to our developing a sense of ourselves. With nine of us, it required real cooperation and attention for everyone to feel heard, but we managed. It was an opportunity to practice not only presence, but also listening.

"But I'm too busy to cook!" is the despairing cry of many overworked parents.

Take heart. The food itself need not be home cooked (although fresh food lovingly prepared is no doubt the best), nor does it need to be prepared by one person. You can order in. Or go out. Or cook together. Make it a democratic event, asking everyone to participate. The point is to create the time for healing your bodies and your spirits. Let it be a time of sharing ideas, stories, events, and being present. Let it be a time to stop the clock and *be here now!*

TUNE IN, NOT OUT

Paying attention and being aware are fundamental to living the intuitive life. Your children start out with this natural, intense presence of mind, but eventually they learn to tune it out. The world will try to teach them this soon enough, but don't let them learn it from you. Exercise your awareness, first with yourself and then with your children. Meditate. Pay attention. Be interested in and aware of your kids. You may have to fight for time in order to keep yourself aware instead of getting swept away in the endless "to do" lists of life, but for both your sake and that of your children, it's essential.

Start right now by doing what I did on the porch that day. Take in a big, long, luxurious breath and return to the moment. Realize all you have is this moment, and refuse to let your ruminations over yesterday or your fears and anxieties of tomorrow steal it away.

Tool A PRESENT FOR YOU

When you are overworked, buried alive in things to do and have no time to do them, you will find it very hard to be patient with anything, let alone with your children. Parenting these days is a full-time job that most of us juggle on top of our full-time professions, leaving us stressed, strained, and moving in hyperdrive. This is precisely the time to do the following exercise. You can do it sitting down or standing up, with your eyes closed.

> Place both feet flat on the ground or floor and let out a long, slow exhale.
>
> Imagine everything that is pressing down on you draining out of your body and into the ground through the soles of your feet. Then, very slowly, place your left hand over your heart and your right hand over your belly. Take in a long, luxurious breath while repeating silently to yourself the following affirmation: I am present. Repeat it again as you breathe out.

Do this slowly five times whenever you feel overwhelmed or are in need of space. Avoid the tendency to rush through this exercise even though you feel you must. Doing this entire exercise *very* slowly takes only four minutes at most and will expand the sense of time you operate in. Four minutes of quieting your nervous system and nurturing yourself can save you hours of wasted anxiety, sudden blowups, potential confrontations, and costly oversights. This brief centering exercise will also alleviate pressure and allow you to engage with your children in a more loving and peaceful way.

Tool TAKE TWENTY

Allow twenty minutes just to be with, play with, talk with, and listen to your child every day. This time can even be broken into two ten-minute segments, one in the morning and one in the evening, but try to allow twenty minutes altogether.

Tool ELEVEN WAYS TO BE IN THE MOMENT

1. When you leave work, *leave work*.
2. Go for a walk with your child, holding hands if possible.
3. Have a family meal (preferably home cooked) with everyone present at least once a week.
4. Have story time after dinner at least once a month. Tell your children stories from your childhood. Tell them stories from your parents' childhood as well. Let your children ask questions, and follow their line of curiosity.
5. Don't take phone calls during dinner.
6. Don't take work phone calls in the evening or on weekends (or at least during predesignated hours set aside for family).
7. Tell your children a bedtime story that you make up.
8. Keep one day a week free to rest, relax, and connect with one another.
9. Do projects together with your kids:
    Plant a garden.
    Do yardwork.
    Paint their room.

Decorate cookies.

Bake a pie.

10. Avoid television as a substitute for true together time.

11. Turn off the radio and have conversations instead.

More Tools FOR INCREASING PRESENCE

Sit down in front of an open window and simply enjoy the view for five minutes a day.

Today:

* Notice one new thing about your children.
* Notice one new thing about your partner.
* Notice one new thing in your neighborhood.

This week:

* Notice one new thing at work.
* Notice one new thing about yourself.
* Identify what wastes your time, and ask yourself what you can do to change this. Also ask yourself if you are willing to change it.

Reflections

1. Are you meditating regularly? What difference, if any, has it made in your awareness?

_____

_____

_____

2. Have you practiced the thumb-forefinger stress buster? What results have you had in using this technique?

_____

_____

_____

3. What was your most recent quality experience with your children?

_____

_____

_____

4. What was your most recent quality experience with your partner? Or a good friend if a single parent? With your parent(s)? With yourself?

_____

_____

_____

5. Is it difficult for you to make the time for and be fully present to your family? If so, what do you fear?

_____

_____

_____

6. Name your three favorite ways to spend quality time alone with your children.

_____

_____

_____

7. What differences in the energies of your family have you noticed or experienced since upgrading the quality of your presence with them?

_____

_____

_____

8. What must you do or eliminate to increase your presence in the moment?

_____

_____

_____

9. Have you noticed any shifts in your children since becoming more present to them?

_____

_____

_____

10. Have you had any new intuitive insights regarding your family since becoming more present? If so, what are they?

_____

_____

_____

THREE

The Heart of the Matter

When my mother was young she suffered a severe case of rheumatic fever, which caused her to gradually lose her hearing in both ears. By the time I was born the loss was noticeable, so I grew up with a mother who was nearly deaf. My mother took the loss of hearing in stride. She used to say, "It's not a problem for me because Divine Spirit gives us two ways to listen—one with our ears and the other, more important way with our hearts." In our family, listening with the heart was a priority. "It's interesting," my mother would say. "When you listen with your heart, your ears work better, too."

Listening with the heart gave us an insightful and intuitive perspective from the very beginning. It influenced the way we took in information. Listening from the heart helped us focus on becoming aware of not only the *content* of information, but its *intent*, its essence, as well. The way I learned to listen from the heart was twofold: first by example, by noticing the way my mother listened to her own heart, and second by the way I was listened to. Though at times my mother struggled to hear my words, I always felt as though she were keenly interested in hearing the message behind them. In other words, I felt heard. At times when we spoke to her, she even closed her eyes and felt our communication energetically. Her heart-based orientation of listening opened an intuitive pathway among all my family members, one that conveyed connection and communication where words failed to register. This intuitive pathway was there even when we weren't speaking. It was as though the family dialogue shifted up an octave and we conversed on a purer, telepathic channel.

Intuitive knowing is actually the art and practice of listening with the heart, for it is there that the voice of inner wisdom speaks. I believe we all start out in life listening to this inner heart-based awareness. Just reflect on how children are so keen in their perceptions and are absorbing everything that comes their way, both content and intent, in its entirety. For example, notice how babies will naturally relax around people who are at ease with them, while they fuss or scream their heads off with people who may smile and coo but are really uncomfortable with them or afraid. They feel the difference in their hearts. Kids pick up absolutely everything that is "in the air." Good or bad, I have seen kids register the truth of a situation faster than the adults around them.

I recall when I was about five years old, coming home from kindergarten and entering the house only to feel a great sense of dread, of sadness, wondering and worrying about what was wrong. Even though there were no obvious signs of trouble, my heart felt something was not quite right. That evening my grandmother, who lived with us, suddenly had a stroke in the backyard.

I'll never forget how, when the ambulance came to get her, I wasn't surprised. I had felt something was about to happen even though I wasn't sure what! Now I knew. It was Grandma. I don't know whether she knew she was sick, or whether my parents knew she was ill, or whether it was a surprise to them. Or to Grandma. All I know is that it wasn't a surprise to me.

Tapping into this inner resource of wisdom begins in the heart. Heart-based wisdom guides us to a broader, deeper perspective and understanding of things. It brings our attention to the unseen subtle aspects of life and directs us toward a more creative, more loving, more insightful approach to life's difficulties.

TRUSTING YOUR HEART

We all feel heart-based connections from time to time because it is our nature to do so. The problem arises when we tune out or doubt this inner sense of awareness, instead surrendering to the world of outside appearances and opinions.

Many people fear having a different perspective from that of others. Even when their heart gives them clear guidance, they will often discount or ignore its message. My husband used to amuse himself by playing a goofy game he made up called Ten-Fifteen. When Patrick went to parties he would ask other guests, "What time do you have?" No matter what the answer was, Patrick would answer, "That's funny, my watch says it's ten-fifteen." Then he would observe how many people would question the accuracy of their own watches before questioning his. The average was sometimes as high as eight out of ten people! It just goes to show how easily people are thrown into doubt about what they know, believing that someone else knows better instead.

This can be especially true for children unless you teach them otherwise. They need to learn from you that it's important to tune in to and trust their hearts and their inner guidance and not be afraid to express what they feel, even if it contradicts what others tell them. When you teach kids to listen to their hearts and honor what they know, you are affirming their intuition.

When Sabrina was only three years old she attended prekindergarten. A naturally spontaneous girl when it comes to following her heart, because we've always encouraged her to do so, she never hesitates in expressing what she feels. For example, one day Sabrina's preschool teacher said she had to tell me a story about an experience she'd had with Sabrina. She had had a major argument with her husband that morning and in her agitated state was having a hard time dealing with the class. Finally it reached such a point that she put the entire class in the corner to take a "time-out." There they sat, hanging their heads in shame for several minutes, when suddenly Sabrina whispered something to the other children. They all nodded their heads in silent, enthusiastic agreement. A moment later Sabrina stood up, crept up to the teacher's desk, and whispered, "Ms. Agnes, we are all feeling fine in the corner. Would you like to sit with us in the corner until you feel better, too?"

Sabrina smiled meekly, tiptoed back to her corner, and sat down once again. The teacher burst out laughing, feeling as though she had been caught. She set the children free from their time-out and took a break herself.

The teacher, recognizing Sabrina's grasp of the situation, laughed when she recounted the story. She was not her usual self that day, and she admired Sabrina's ability to feel and say what the real problem was.

It's important to notice that children do listen from their heart naturally. What we as parents need to do is follow their good example and affirm to them how *wise* this is, even if the world around them has forgotten how to.

If children aren't censored or subjected to an environment where intuitive heart-based awareness is discouraged, if they are allowed to feel and freely express their heart-based feelings, they will establish and strengthen a very solid and natural connection to inner guidance. They will remain conscious of their important connection in the scheme of things, and they will look to their hearts for verification.

IT BEGINS WITH LISTENING

Learning to listen from the heart begins with learning to listen. I recently heard a statistic on a radio program that said most people hear only 50 percent of what is said and only 20 percent of that is retained for more than an hour. When it comes to being a busy parent, I wonder what percentage of real attention is available for listening to a child?

Real listening means just that—not interrupting, fixing, solving, cutting off, or shutting down your children before they fully express what they have to say. Don't let impatience move you to speak before they are finished. The great majority of all relationship problems arise out of the frustration of not being heard, and this includes a relationship with your own intuition.

When your children are upset or angry, or simply need to share something with you, practice giving them your full attention. If they are having squabbles with their siblings, listen to each child, one at a time. Make a rule in your home that when your children are angry or need to speak, they can express everything without censorship or interruption, on the condition that it be delivered in a calm tone of voice. They cannot scream or insult anyone while expressing their feelings. This doesn't mean that you must agree with what they are angry about. It means only that you care enough to allow your children to express their feelings fully.

I realize it can be very hard to listen to your children at certain times, especially if you are overtired or in a hurry. Unfortunately this is usually when they approach you to talk. Because it is often inconvenient or impossible to truly listen to your children at these times, make an agreement in advance to actively listen to them at some prearranged time, perhaps before bedtime, when you can. Then honor that agreement. Pick the most realistic time of day to be able to fully listen to what your children have to say, without interruption, and then do.

This decision takes great effort and patience, but it is very worthwhile and a terrific catalyst for awakening intuition. We all need to feel and express our feelings, anger included, as well as be listened to, to feel balanced and grounded. This ritual will clear the air, keep you in touch with your inner voice and your children's true needs, and help build a real and solid relationship with your own "inner teacher."

BE HONEST

Having an open heart is central to intuitive awareness, and no heart is more open than a child's. Our job as parents is to keep their hearts open by having open hearts ourselves. We need to help them believe in themselves and not doubt what they feel, by first believing in ourselves and trusting what we feel. We need to help them find the courage to stick to what is true for them and not ignore it by sticking to what is true for us and not ignoring our own feelings. One way we can do this is by being completely honest and sharing our feelings truthfully.

Once I had a client, Martin, who came for a reading on the suggestion of his wife, because he was quite frustrated over his relationship with his daughter. Martin was a very intellectual man, highly uncomfortable with any outward expression of emotion. He strove to keep himself on an even keel at all times and did everything in his power to keep his world pleasant, no matter what. He thought that by accomplishing this, he was creating a loving environment. More truthfully, he was exercising control.

In his quest to avoid any unpleasantness he found that he was alienating his five-year-old daughter, Gloria. She disregarded him most of the time, often speaking to him rudely and making it clear that she preferred the company of Mommy. And she loved to make a scene of it.

He said to me, "I don't get it, Sonia. Gloria and her mom fight constantly, yet when I show up and am friendly she's contemptuous. She has no respect for me at all, and it's upsetting me. I try not to show it, but it's not working."

It was true. Gloria didn't respect her father much, but there was a reason for it. Gloria was very intuitive and felt instinctively that her dad's superficial "all is well" approach to life was phony. The picture he painted for her wasn't coming from his heart, and she felt it. She could feel that by avoiding confrontation, he was avoiding passion, energy, and maybe life itself, and that included her. At least Mom was real, angry or not, and that made her feel safe.

But Gloria was only five, and she didn't know all this intellectually. She knew only that Dad bothered her. She was simply expressing her own instinct of "I know the real story, you can't fool me!" Martin needed to be more authentic with Gloria and express what was in his heart, which at times would mean showing irritation, enforcing discipline, and setting limits with her. As Martin began to open his heart and express his feelings more honestly, Gloria felt safer and more secure.

A client named Mary Ann came to see me a year ago because her seventeen-year-old son, Ryan, had just been arrested for possession of marijuana. Mary Ann was appalled.

"Sonia, we have provided him with a model home life. I just don't understand it."

"But Mary Ann, I don't see a model home," I answered. "I see a home where you and your husband are completely estranged and barely acknowledge one another, putting up a facade of pleasantries instead."

"Maybe so, but Ryan doesn't know that."

"Oh, really? How could he not know it?"

"We've decided to keep it from him because we didn't want to upset him while he's in high school. We'll deal with our own problems when he leaves for college."

"So you live in two separate worlds, hoping no one will notice or acknowledge it?" I continued.

"Basically, yes. I have my world of horses, and my husband has his world of work. We don't talk a lot, but we're always cordial with each other when we do. It works out."

"Has Ryan ever inquired about your problems?" I probed gently.

"Once, a while back, but we reassured him that we were working things out and doing fine. He forgot all about it after that."

"Well, from what I can tell, he hasn't forgotten about it at all. Quite the opposite. He intuitively feels everything. He's simply decided that since you two have set up a world of denial, and have shut down your hearts, using your interests as a way to do so, why shouldn't he?"

"What do you mean?"

"I mean that Ryan has done what you've done. He's fallen out of touch with his heart and set up a world of appearances, just as you have. After all, if you two aren't really truthful, not really there, why should *he* be? He just chose marijuana as his distraction of choice. Unfortunately it's illegal, and he got caught."

To say that Mary Ann was surprised was putting it mildly. After Ryan was placed on probation, I suggested counseling all around and urged that they make a sincere attempt to get to the heart of the matter and speak truthfully with one another about their lives and the need for changes.

Mary Ann called six months later to tell me that she and her husband were separating and that Ryan was preparing to leave for college.

All three of them had "come clean," so to speak, after months of intense family counseling. "We are having hard times with so much change, but our relationships are more honest, which I think makes Ryan feel more secure. At least he isn't stoned anymore."

THE FAMILY MEETING

Perhaps this ritual more than any other has assisted my family in opening our hearts and connecting with our intuition. Our family meeting is a weekly gathering where all members of the family share with one another our most heartfelt feelings and thoughts. They are held on Sunday evenings after dinner and usually last from fifteen minutes to an hour. During the meeting each of us takes a turn to "check in" and share what's in our hearts. A check-in consists of expressing how we feel, what is troubling us, what is challenging us, and what we need from the other family members to support us. This is also a time to bring up any problems we may be having with one another and air our differences in an atmosphere that is safe and supportive even when the communications are difficult. This gives each of us an opportunity to air our complaints and ask for changes without suffering any negative consequences for being honest. It is a time of honest sharing, clarity, support, and receiving. These meetings allow for all of us to connect with our own hearts and better understand the hearts of one another. They establish goodwill and safety among us and prevent misunderstandings from piling up. They also help set up the habit of honest, heartfelt communicating at home.

As parents we can do a lot to awaken our children's intuition by turning to the heart. Recognize and acknowledge what is real, both seen and unseen, and encourage your kids to do the same. After all, they sense the truth; you need to acknowledge it, too.

As you work to help your children awaken their intuition, realize that this doesn't mean you want them to focus on some "otherworldly" place or experience. Quite the opposite. Truly heightened perception is the understanding that comes from recognizing that we are all spiritual beings who are connected to one another by sharing the same breath. We must pay attention to what we experience and be aware of how it affects us and others. And to do that we must turn our awareness inward and look for our truth. True intuition is not a pursuit of messages from outer space. It is developing a keen sense of how energy, seen and unseen, affects us all by focusing "in here," in your heart, where your true self, your soul, resides. Only when we listen with both head and heart and express what we feel to be honest and true will we have a clear and complete sense of real direction in life.

Listening with the heart is the very foundation of intuitive living. When we tune inward, into the inner voice in our hearts, we tap into an unlimited resource of Higher Intelligence, guidance, and direction. Our heart is the well of insight, bright ideas, and sudden solutions. It is here in our hearts that we become aware of the subtle hidden side of things and so often the "truth" of what we are dealing with in life.

One of the greatest problems I see in my work with clients is that so many people have overvalued their heads and have lost touch with their hearts. Our intellectual side is wonderful for informing us about the visible world, but it can lose its way on the unseen plane. The visible world can be very deceiving indeed. To our eyes we appear separate and different from one another. To our intellects we appear superior and inferior to one another. To our logic we appear threatened and even endangered by one another. So we withdraw. We put up defenses. We become fearful and suspicious. We lose our confidence, which dims our awareness, leading us into an ever more isolated and spiritually bankrupt state.

The spiritual world is heart based. It reveals the hidden truth behind appearances and shows us our connection to one another. It shows us our need for one another. It opens our hearts and then our hands, moving us to reach out and touch one another. This is a truer world than the one of appearances. This is the world where cooperation and creativity can thrive, making it a safer world than the one our talking heads have created.

TUNING IN TO THE HEART

Listening to your heart or the voice of the soul begins with practice. It may take several weeks of concentrated effort on your part to get into the habit of tuning in to your heart for direction. Here are several tools to help you begin.

Tool LISTENING TO THE HEART

Every time you need guidance, counsel, direction, or simply reassurance, close your eyes, take in a few deep, cleansing breaths, then place your attention directly on your heart. Allow your focus to rest there quietly for a moment or two, then ask your heart to guide you. Trust whatever feelings come up. Don't censor or discount a thing. If nothing comes to you from the heart immediately, don't worry. Relax. Remain open and patient. Guidance will come before you know it.

Tool BREATHING AS YOU LISTEN

My teachers taught me that it is much easier to tune in to your heart, as well as listen to others from the heart, when you breathe. So often miscommunication occurs because everyone is holding his or her breath, making it almost impossible to truly hear anything someone else is saying. Whenever you want to deliver a heartfelt communication, or even to get in touch with what is in your own heart, begin by taking three or four deep, cleansing breaths and then returning to a calm, steady breathing pattern.

Tool HAND ON THE HEART

A favorite technique in our family for listening with the heart is actually placing a hand over the heart, letting it rest there as we speak and listen to one another. This is our signal to one another that we have something important to say and that we want to be truly heard. This is an especially effective technique for settling arguments and opening up troubled communication.

Reflections

1. Was anyone in your childhood home available to listen to you with the heart? When?

_____

_____

_____

2. Were you ever conscious of the difference between listening with the heart and not listening with the heart?

_____

_____

_____

3. Were you freely able to express your innermost, heartfelt feelings as a child?

_____

_____

_____

4. If you were censored as a child, are you still censoring yourself?

_____

_____

_____

5. Have you tried using the hand over your heart technique? What results did you have?

_____

_____

_____

6. Have you tried the breathing as you listen technique? What were the results?

_____

_____

_____

7. Have you had a family meeting? What happened?

_____

_____

_____

8. Is your heart opening? How does it feel? Has your family noticed?

_____

_____

_____

9. What shifts has listening with your heart brought about in your family?

_____

_____

_____

FOUR

Creating a Sacred Home

Once you begin raising your awareness and opening your heart, it is important to examine the energy and atmosphere of your home to ensure that it too encourages intuitive expression and provides a spiritually healthy environment for you and your children.

A few years ago during an extremely stressful renovation of our very first home, Patrick and I were having a great deal of difficulty getting along. We were both trying our best to handle the stress, but the renovation was moving too slowly, the costs were soaring out of sight, the workmen were not doing the job as well as we wanted them to, and the disruption prevented us from finding anyplace to go to recover our equilibrium. Every day brought new disagreements, each more serious than the day before; and worn out from the cumulative problems, we were soon at war.

Tension seemed to hang in the air. It got to the point where we were in perfectly fine spirits until we crossed the threshold of our home, and then instantly we would fall into a bad mood. We were all absolutely miserable, not only Patrick and me, but the girls as well.

During this disabling period, Sabrina, who was two years old at the time, cried, screamed, hollered, and threw a fit every night, just as soon as we went to bed. Often, no matter what we did, she wouldn't sleep through the night. Finally it occurred to me that she was trying to get our attention. She was trying to tell us how much the toxic energy of the house was affecting her; the only way she could get us to notice her was at midnight, when everything else had settled down.

Sabrina was right. Our house *had* taken on a very bleak atmosphere. It had become so stressful, so unsettled, and so out of order that it failed to provide any of us with the basics of a home: safety, serenity, and protection from the world. The energy caused all of us to feel defensive, volatile, and threatened instead. Our house was not a place to retreat to; it had become a place to retreat *from*. We needed to do something and do it immediately. This was an emergency!

Patrick and I called a truce from our battles and discussed the need to create some sanctuary in the midst of the crisis. We decided to concentrate all our renovation efforts on the bedrooms and finish them up as quickly as possible, so that at least then we would have some place to go for peace and quiet. This important decision made a tremendous difference in the way we were all feeling. Having a peaceful corner to retreat to in the midst of the confusion allowed us to relax, regain perspective, and avoid "psychic overload"–induced squabbles. Even the girls seemed to calm down a bit once in their own settled rooms.

It is interesting to me now to remember how obsessed Patrick and I were with removing all the toxic materials in that house so the children would be safe. We stripped the lead paint. We removed the asbestos and pulled out all flammable wiring. But in being so focused on the physical elements of toxicity, we failed to consider the nonphysical toxic conditions. The atmosphere of disruption was just as toxic as asbestos or lead. Arguing, disorder, stress, change—all lent our home a feeling of great dis-ease.

It took effort and awareness on our part, but eventually we were able to turn the energy around. Very intentionally we began blessing the rooms and asking the Universe to restore tranquillity. Very methodically we played soothing classical and ambient music during the day and kept the house as clean as was possible in a construction zone. Eventually, after several months, the energy in the house began to improve significantly. We began to experience a more peaceful and healing vibration. What a relief!

With the restoration of tranquil energy in our home, the kids settled down. Sabrina, who had had difficulty sleeping and frequent nightmares, began to sleep peacefully through the night. Sonia's spontaneous outbursts lessened. Patrick and I reestablished goodwill between us and started enjoying one another once again. Finally the job was finished. There was no doubt about it. Having not only a beautiful but a *peaceful* home made a huge difference in the quality of all our lives, and it was a difference we were now committed to maintaining.

ENERGY AND PLACE

This experience made me very aware of how important the energy we live in actually is. Just as people have certain energy and vibrations, so do places. The energy of a church or synagogue will be very different from that of a subway station, just as the energy of one place of worship may be very different from that of another. We are subjected to all kinds of energy all day long that we can't control, and this is especially true for kids. Their schools have a certain energy, as do their school buses, day care centers, and after-school jobs. With so many divorced families, Mom's place has one feeling and Dad's place another. And every one of these places has energy that influences our children.

Ask yourself what kind of energy your home has. Is it a calm and tranquil place? Do your children feel safe and protected from the world there? Is it peaceful? Is it clean and organized? When they come home, can they let down their guard and feel secure? Can they open up their hearts and expand into reverie and imagination in relatively relaxed conditions? Or do they have to hunker down, run for cover, and walk on eggshells?

SACRED SPACE

I have witnessed so many different kinds of vibrations in homes, both in the course of my work as an intuitive and in the course of pursuing my hobby—exploring old houses. What I have seen tells me that many, many people are unconscious about how energy affects them and have no idea how much their spirits need a sacred space to dwell in, for the sake of themselves and their children. It is truly alarming for me to realize just how many people live in the intuitive equivalent of a toxic waste dump. This should not be acceptable. We, and especially our children, are sensitive beings. We are just as much in need of peace and tranquillity as any other delicate creature. We need to commit ourselves to creating such a sacred environment for ourselves and for them.

I was first introduced to the power of sacred space while studying with Dr. Trenton Tully as a teenager. He gave lessons in metaphysics and spirituality in a magnificent old mansion in Denver. When I first walked through the front door of that mansion, I was immediately taken with the smell of incense wafting through the rooms, with the beauty of the architecture and the furniture, the glow of the candles, and mostly with the realization that I was in a very special, holy place. The aura was as clear as a summer sunrise. The energy was as calm as the still waters on a lake at dusk. The atmosphere was serene and soothing and made me feel very secure, as though I were in a place where nothing could harm me.

Dr. Tully told me the place was healing because of all the intention put into its being a healing place. He emphasized the need to dwell in serenity in order to help me grow spiritually and awaken our intuitive hearts. "It's very hard to be aware and open," he'd say, "if you find yourself constantly subjected to confusing, negative, and disruptive energy. Insist, therefore, on creating for yourself a calm and harmonious environment to live in."

The first and most obvious way to create a calm and peaceful sacred space in your home is to keep it clean and organized and filled with things that offer beauty and bring comfort to your spirit. Dr. Tully taught me that everything is composed of energy and that everything we own absorbs our energy. This can be felt in Grandpa's chair or Aunt

Mary's shawl. It can be felt with Dad's gold watch or your own favorite childhood toy. The affection that we feel for things is integrated into the very things themselves and can be felt, which is why heirlooms are so prized. The vibration they give off is usually charged with tremendous sentimental affection. The same holds true for negative energy, however. It, too, will linger in an atmosphere, bringing down anyone who comes into contact with its dreary and brittle vibration. That's why, if we and our children are living in messy, unloved, neglected disarray, we will come to resent it. First the ugly environment itself discharges bad energy, and the resentment we feel because of it keeps recycling the negativity, further compounding its toxicity and setting off a vicious cycle. The best cure for this problem is to clean and clear out or throw away all that isn't necessary, or used, or comforting to your spirit. If it's ugly, irritating, broken-down, or useless, get rid of it! Given the effect it has on you, it isn't worth keeping.

CLEAN UP, CLEAR OUT

I was visiting my friend Francie, a veteran packrat, a few years ago. When I arrived, much to my dismay, I found her house to be an absolute disaster of unloved, outgrown toys, furniture, and junk. As much as I loved her, it was really hard for me to be there.

She had three kids, ages four to eleven, and all three seemed to show no interest whatsoever in any of the mountain of useless stuff lying about. During my entire visit, however, they did endure several shouting rounds a day of "Clean up this place!" from Mom, who felt my discomfort. The household atmosphere was irritable, unpleasant, and extremely uncomfortable to be in, and she knew it.

The effort it took to navigate through the mess was really annoying and kept everyone from enjoying one another. The negativity it created hung in the air like a cloud.

Had Francie simply cleared out the unwanted things (and energy), it would have made a huge difference in lightening up the atmosphere in the home and making it a much more pleasant place. It was a suggestion I made on my way to the airport as Francie was once again apologizing for everyone's bad manners. It was something she had already considered but had yet to do.

"I know you are right, Sonia. I don't know why I haven't done it already. Lazy, perhaps, or a fear that I might need it someday?" she said. "I don't know."

"Well, if you did get rid of the junk and clean the place up, it would raise the energy in your home to a more pleasant level, which I'm sure you would all appreciate," I answered. "Why don't you start by donating what you no longer need to people who could really use it."

"That's a good idea! Maybe I will."

I visited Francie a year later. Much to my surprise (and relief), this time the house was clutter free and the vibration was much more peaceful. As I walked in Francie said, "Sonia, we took your advice and cleaned up this place. I just couldn't stand it anymore. Neither could my husband or the kids. Once we got started, we couldn't stop. We cleaned out everything and donated it to the Salvation Army. It felt great! Having learned our lesson, our new house rule is, For every new thing that comes in, one old, useless thing goes out. The energy around here feels a lot better, don't you think?"

"It certainly does," I said, dropping my bag and relaxing.

Francie's idea of keeping things moving is an excellent way to clear energy and restore tranquillity, and one I continue to suggest to clients and students all the time. By practicing this simple rule, you'll never become bogged down or energetically drained by having to deal with unnecessary stuff. Try it. It works.

PLAY AREAS, PEACEFUL AREAS

Another way to create a peaceful aura is to designate certain areas in which to play and allow disorder, leaving other areas for quiet and calm. If you are short of rooms for this plan, you can designate times for disorder and play and other times for calm. In our house the basement is the place for creative disorder, where the girls can practice their arts and crafts or play with their toys and be as messy as they want, which is important for creative play. But the bedrooms are designated for order and calm. This doesn't prevent the girls from being creative in their rooms. It only requires that their rooms be kept somewhat organized so that they can sleep in relatively peaceful energy.

I'm sure every parent of a sloppy kid or teenager groans over this suggestion, thinking it's impossible to convince their kid to clean up. My suggestion is rather than simply enforcing rules of order, explain to your children how the energy of places can influence how we feel, then invite them to notice for themselves how true this is. For example, ask them about their favorite places and why they are favorites, as well as places that bother them and how that energy feels as well. Encourage them to notice how their own rooms affect them. Is there a soothing quality to their space, or is it draining? The key is to allow children to create their own system of organization. Your idea of calm and comfort may not be the same as theirs. Ask them how you can help them. Do they need drawers, shelves, a desk? Can you help provide them?

Tool CREATING A SACRED ALTAR

A wonderful way to create a healing vibration in the home is to create a sacred altar. This altar should be set up in a corner of the home where it will be left undisturbed. It can be set up on a table or placed on a small box. It can even be set up on the floor if it won't be in the way.

> On your altar place beloved objects, photos, and talismans of those people and things you love. These may include religious icons, family photos, even articles from nature—anything that lifts your spirits and moves you into your heart. You may also want to place fresh flowers, candles, or incense on your altar. Let the altar serve as a site for contemplation, reverie, meditation, and prayer. This sacred spot will become charged with the alchemy of peace and tranquillity and will serve as a place of healing in your home.

(Usually a personal altar is such a compelling thing that once children see it, they want to contribute to it or create one for themselves.)

Tool MUSIC AND AROMATHERAPY

Another lovely way to create soothing energy in the home is to play calming, meditative, or classical music. It's a known fact that music by Baroque composers such as Bach, Vivaldi, Telemann, or Handel will calm the heartbeat of anyone listening and create an inner state of tranquillity. It's a terrific antidote for some of the more dissonant experiences we encounter during the day.

You can also create a calm and healing atmosphere through the use of aromatherapy. In aromatherapy you fill the home with essential scents that are known to calm and soothe—oils such as lavender, chamomile, and rose oil. Simply put a drop or two of an essential oil on a light bulb ring (found where essential oils are sold) in each room. The warmth of the light bulb then diffuses the oil, filling the room with a beautiful aroma and energy. Aromatherapy works directly on the nervous system, calming and soothing.

Tool THE TRANQUILLITY ROOM

Another great way to create healing energy in the home is to pick one place in the house where no one is ever allowed to argue or even to enter the space in an angry mood. Designate this space as a sanctuary. If you live in a small apartment or there is no room, choose the bathroom. It's a natural choice anyway. I've had hundreds of adults tell me that they used to hide in the bathroom as kids when arguments broke out or they needed some privacy. It worked so well that they still do it.

Tool PUT LIVE THINGS IN EACH ROOM

Another way to create a healing energy in the home is to place something living in each room—potted and flowering plants or pets such as fish, birds, turtles, hamsters, or gerbils. The point is to have a home that hosts the beauty and vibration of nature. Animals and plants fill a house with love and light. Both have a very high, clear vibration and will help to clear away sadness, grief, anger, and depression.

Of course, I don't mean to suggest having too many live animals! This goes back to my first dictum—order. Have only as many plants and pets as you can care for. Dying plants and ailing animals create just the opposite of the effect you want.

BE SENSITIVE

A safe and energetically clear and gentle home environment includes an atmosphere that is clear of addiction, chronic rage and anger, dishonesty, fear, and abuse.

I have seen so many joyous and delightful children, children who are bright, creative, and keenly intuitive, diminish like shrinking violets in households where dysfunction, stress, and terror are the name of the game. As parents we are spiritually required to take a look in the mirror and ask ourselves if we are doing our best to provide our children with energetically safe and grounded homes. I cannot count how many wounded adults I have encountered in my work who have come to me to recover the loss of safety and protection they experienced as children. These are the adult children of alcoholics, rage-aholics, and workaholics who ignored the psychic atmosphere their children lived in and, worse, created a toxic one instead. I have seen so many adults in despair, not knowing what or whom to trust because they grew up in chaos and had no one to trust as children. Without trust we cannot connect to our heart wisdom and awaken intuitively.

The atmosphere our children live in will determine more than anything whether or not they will open their hearts, follow their truth, and be themselves in life or whether they will simply become actors and actresses, taking on a superficial veneer designed to protect themselves from the chaos and abuse they suffer in their own homes.

BE FAIR

Kids are very vulnerable. Because they are so dependent on us, it is easy for adults not to give them a vote in what happens to them. It is easy to ignore how our problems affect them. But just because we don't tell them that we have problems doesn't mean they don't *feel* them. They do, and it scares them because they usually can't do anything about it.

However, while all parents want to create a safe and sacred home for their children, attempting to eliminate all family problems is not the best approach. It's an impossible task—life is full of problems. Instead, have the integrity and fairness of heart to communicate with your children when you do have problems and let them know that *they* are not the problem. Don't avoid acknowledging problems or, worse yet, use your children as scapegoats when problems arise. This will only confuse them because they intuitively feel everything. The problem is that they may not always interpret what they feel correctly. If you are troubled but won't acknowledge it or seek help, they will assume it's their fault and take on guilt and shame.

I had a client who was divorcing his wife after a three-year cold war. Though they were barely civil, nothing was ever discussed with their children, who were four and eight years old. These kids felt the tension in the air so intensely that one developed anxiety attacks and the other took to chewing his fingernails down to the quick.

My client finally did move out and never fully explained to the children the reasons for the divorce. He told me his kids are emotionally devastated and no longer trust him, themselves, or anyone, and he can't figure out why.

"I was only trying to protect them," he said. "Why would they want to know about my problems with their mom?"

But he wasn't protecting them. He was only avoiding what made him uncomfortable. This family is now sorting itself out in counseling, but they have a long way to go.

If your household is tense, uptight, unhappy, toxic, angry, unsafe, or insecure, ask yourself why. And more important, ask yourself why you are willing to settle for such a disabling and disheartening condition for yourselves and your children. If you are avoiding doing the work of finding your own peace, now is the time to begin. For your sake and that of your kids, start finding solutions.

If you have addictions, seek help.
If you have marital problems, seek help.
If you are in a spiritual crisis, seek help.
If you are lonely, exhausted, overextended, isolated, be gentle with yourself . . . and *seek help*.

Part of the difficulty of parenting today is that the work it involves, on top of the demands of a full-time job, leaves little room to nurture ourselves as individuals. And when your own spirit is neglected, everyone feels it and suffers for it. The renewal and benefit of support, community, and friendship for yourself gives you the energy to offer the same to your family.

Be fair with your kids. Let them know the real source of your trouble. Don't let them become scapegoats or leave them to parent you. It isn't fair if you do, and it will shut down their open hearts. And if you already have, apologize. They will appreciate it.

Go to church. Go to a counselor. Go to a friend. Join a creativity class or an exercise class. Go to God in prayer. Go to the mirror and find the self-love and integrity to do *whatever* it takes to create the peace you need and deserve, so that your children will grow up in a home that provides them with the sacred space and protection from the world that they deserve.

There is something profoundly disabling to our souls when we live in a relentless atmosphere of toxic, negative, stressed, angry, disruptive energy. It wears us out, makes us sick, desensitizes our children, and disconnects us all from our spiritual centers. It shuts down our awareness and cuts off our capacity to feel and follow our inner wisdom.

In America this condition is epidemic. As parents we need to shake ourselves out of the tendency to accept such toxic conditions, both for ourselves and for our children. We would never consider living in a poisonous atmosphere, yet we accept living in poisonous energy. We need to turn this condition around. There is a Chinese saying: "When one becomes so accustomed to danger that it feels normal, the soul is lost."

We need to police our intuitive environments. We need to become energy cops. And we need to grant our children the right to do the same. We need to claim for ourselves a calm and loving atmosphere, at least in our own homes. We must insist on this place of spiritual renewal, not as a luxury, but as a foundation of intuitive health and well-being.

We owe this to our children. We owe this to ourselves.

Tool AIR FRESHENER

One of the most frightening situations a child endures is the tension and anxiety that comes with a disagreement or an argument between their parents. They become scared and feel insecure. Since relationships inevitably bring up conflict at times, it's not possible (or even necessarily desirable) to avoid an occasional collision of opinion.

If constant disagreements or tension are polluting your home, open the windows and doors and allow in a moment or two of fresh air and energy. Then light a dried sage smudge stick (available in metaphysical bookstores) and let the sweet smoke fill the rooms. Ask all the arguing parties to go for a walk around the block until they cool off.

Tool BLESS YOUR HOUSE

Have all family members light a candle, then together walk from room to room, blessing your home. As you bless the living room, ask that it bring you pleasant company and positive memories. As you bless the kitchen, ask that it nurture your bodies and souls. As you bless the bedrooms, ask that they soothe and heal you as you sleep and bring you pleasant dreams.

If you are uncomfortable doing this, then simply thank God, in your own way as a family, for providing you with a safe haven and sanctuary. Ask for continued protection and blessings in your home.

Tool BEAUTIFY YOUR SURROUNDINGS

The human spirit thrives on harmony, beauty, and balance. Paint your home in tranquil tones. Bring in fresh flowers. Arrange your furniture in pleasant configurations. Eliminate clutter and disorder. Burn incense. Hang beautiful pictures and mirrors to enhance the light. Open the blinds and shades and let in the light. If your home is naturally dark, hang mirrors and burn full-spectrum light bulbs. Light keeps energy moving. Love yourselves enough to care and to create harmony in every room.

Tool DANCE AND SING

When a person dances and sings, spirit enters the body. A home filled with song and dance is a home filled with grace, so put on your favorite music and let your feet take over.

Tool QUIET

Loud and dissonant noises are disturbing to the spirit. Practice keeping the volume of the house at a pleasant level. This includes the volume of televisions, stereos, and voices. Be conscious of how delicate we are and how we need a certain amount of calm to tune inward.

Reflections

1. How would you describe the tone and energy of your home?

_____

_____

_____

2. Is it clutter free and organized? Where does clutter need attention?

_____

_____

_____

3. If not, how does this make you and other family members feel?

_____

_____

_____

4. Can you designate play areas and calm areas in your home? Where?

_____

_____

_____

5. Have you created a personal altar? If so, how does this affect you?

_____

_____

_____

6. Have you shared this idea with your children? How have they responded to this suggestion?

_____

_____

_____

7. Have you experimented with aromatherapy in your home?

_____

_____

_____

8. If so, have you noticed how it affects you and the other members of your family?

_____

_____

_____

9. Have you experimented with some form of classical music in your home? What kind?

_____

_____

_____

10. Have you noticed an increase in awareness and sensitivity in your children since you began consciously to raise the energy level?

_____

_____

_____

11. Does your home have plants? Animals? Fish? Live things in each room? Do you sense how these living energies influence the atmosphere?

_____

_____

_____

12. Is your own personal energy clear? Are you emotionally free of clutter?

_____

_____

_____

13. The energy you personally put out into the atmosphere of your home is the most influential of all. Is your energy calm and healing? Or are you toxic, angry, and tense? If so, what do you intend to do about it in order to heal?

_____

_____

_____

REMINDERS
Are you:
   Meditating daily?
   Simplifying your schedule?
   Tuning in to your heart?
   Keeping your house clutter free and serene?

Embracing Intuition

IN PART II YOU WILL FOCUS on coming to accept intuition as a gift from spirit and begin to welcome it into your life and your home. You will do this in several ways:

1. You will be introduced to the world of energy and vibration and learn to understand its influence in our lives.

2. You will learn creative ways to acknowledge and express intuitive feelings as a part of our spiritual anatomy.

3. You will learn how energy affects us all and explore ways of establishing better personal boundaries and psychic protection for yourself and your children.

4. Finally, you will look at some common blind spots and bad

habits that interrupt the unfolding of your own and your child's intuition and learn techniques that will help overcome this unconscious
tendency.

Hopefully, by the end of this section you will have made the transition
from awakening personal intuitive awareness to awakening intuition in
your children and will be well on your way toward receiving the gifts of
spirit in your home.

✱ FIVE

Awakening to Vibration

The most significant difference between growing up in our household and growing up in those of some of my friends was that the boundaries among the material plane, the emotional plane, and the intuitive plane were nonexistent. We were taught to view everything as being on one plane—the plane of energy.

Being an avid student of metaphysics, my mom taught us something that quantum physicists now corroborate: Everything on our planet comprises energy in motion, and a table, a chair, a plant, and a child are composed of the same essential matter that is energy in motion, although each appears different to our eyes because of the vibratory rate at which it operates. On the mundane level, this translated in our household into our being able to recognize thoughts and emotions as solidly and distinctly as we felt the floor under our feet. My mother would often say to us, "I can feel what you're thinking, so you'd better think straight."

We never felt that simply because something was out of sight it was out of mind. We often tuned in to things at a distance. We might get a feeling Dad was bringing ice cream home to surprise us and arrive home to find that he had. Or that Aunt Emma was going to call and ask us to spend the night, only to have her invitation an hour or so later. Frequently my mother would announce out loud that so-and-so must be thinking about her, because she felt that person pop into her mind. It wasn't unusual for her to stop midsentence, holding one finger up to her lips to silence us while she tuned inward. "Shh!" she'd say, as though listening to some intuitive broadcast. And we would all sit in silence while she tuned in to another frequency.

This sort of tuning in to one another on the intuitive level became a family trademark. Soon enough we all came to recognize each family member's unique vibration. It was as though each of us had our own music or song that we broadcast on a telepathic wavelength, a song that became very familiar and recognizable to each one of us.

WHAT IS A PERSONAL VIBRATION?

My studies have taught me that one's personal vibration is the combined energy of the physical body, the emotional state, and the etheric, or intuitive, consciousness. This synthesis of energy, when in harmony, makes for a grounded, peaceful vibration, like a well-composed piece of music. If, however, any one of the elements of the self is disturbed or out of balance, the personal vibration becomes dissonant, energetically "off-key." To an aware and sensitive person this dissonance can be felt, usually around the heart, chest, or stomach area. Such awareness can alert sensitive parents not only to their own dissonance, but also to that of their child, guiding them to take steps to regain inner balance.

I recall sitting in the kitchen one day after school with a few girlfriends, my two sisters, and my mother, just laughing and talking about the day. All of a sudden my mom shushed us. "Quiet! Something's up."

We all shut up instantly, trying to focus on what she was tuning in to. Abruptly she said, "Where's Anthony?" None of us knew where my brother was, so she continued to concentrate.

"Anthony has been hurt. I feel it!"

Tense, we all sat quietly, wondering exactly what could be going on. No more than ten minutes passed when the phone rang. It was Denver General Hospital. Apparently Anthony had been in a car accident coming home from school. The car he was riding in had been hit from behind, and he had gone right through the windshield. My mom had tuned in to his physical energy at the moment he was hit. It was as though she had been hit, too. Luckily, Anthony had suffered only cuts and bruises. He was stitched up and sent home two hours later.

This incident left a huge impression on me. It taught me just how much and how far our energy travels and can be felt. We are indeed far more than our bodies.

A few years later I had another experience with my mother's telepathic communications. We kids were entering our teen years in the era of rock concerts, dating, and generally spreading our wings. One winter evening my brother Neil set off for a rock concert in Steamboat Springs with his friends. It was a very cold, snowy night, and they traveled sixty miles into the mountains to get there. At one in the morning the phone rang and woke my parents. It was the police, who informed my father that Neil had been in a car wreck and was seriously injured. He had been taken by ambulance to a mountain hospital. His chances for survival didn't look good.

My father was terribly upset and told my mom. At first she was frantic, but then a calm came over her.

"It's not him," she said.

"What?" my dad argued. "They have his driver's license! He's at the hospital. Now hurry up and let's go."

"No, it isn't him. I can feel his vibration. He's fine."

My father ignored her and began to dress quickly, but my mother just sat there, motionless. Ten minutes later, just as my dad was about to leave, the phone rang again. It was Neil, very agitated.

"Dad, I'm at the hospital."

"Are you all right?" my father asked.

"I'm fine, but there was an accident in front of us on the way home. The driver ahead of us must have fallen asleep at the wheel. He lost control of the car, swerved into the other lane, and collided with an oncoming car. It was terrible! We stopped and helped the people until the police came."

"The police just called and told us *you* were the one hurt," my father answered. "They found your driver's license in your coat pocket."

"No, I'm all right, but I put my coat over one of the guys who was injured. My wallet must have been in the pocket. It's a mistake, don't worry. I'm fine."

My dad hung up the phone, greatly relieved and a little shocked over the whole bizarre incident. He turned to my mom and said, "That was Neil. Evidently he's okay."

My mom smiled as she started to cry. "I told you. It *wasn't* his vibration."

WE ALL HAVE A PERSONAL VIBRATION

Every one of us has a personal vibration, just as all of us have an energy field. Children recognize personal vibrations, especially when they're infants. It's how they know you are planning to leave the house before you've even made the final decision to do so. It's why they run to the door before you come home. It's what they are responding to when you are angry or sad or fearful and they cower quietly in the corner. It's what they feel when you are happy, drawing them toward you, wanting to share in the good vibes.

Our personal vibrations, like fingerprints or the sound of our voice, can be felt by really paying attention to and noticing one another. These personal vibrations relay everything about us, physically, emotionally, and psychically—whether we are strong or weak, happy or sad, sick or healthy, whether we are grounded or floating, focused or lost. Even whether we are aware or unconscious.

We attune ourselves to these personal vibrations through the heart. Do you remember when you fell in love? Do you recall times when the phone rang and you *knew* it was (or wasn't) your beloved? What you were tuning in to was a personal vibration. It's like your calling card— as uniquely yours as your personality.

Becoming aware of your personal vibration means teaching yourself to notice and respond to the subtle energies of our being. This awareness originates in the heart, and it takes sensitivity, effort, and attention if you are to succeed. I suggest to my students that becoming aware of a personal vibration is no different from learning to appreciate music. Music to the uneducated ear is a pleasant blur of sound. But with attention and awareness, we can raise our perceptions and begin to discern the individual instruments that blend together to create such beauty.

The beginning of your ability to perceive personal vibration lies in shifting your attention away from your head and the world of thoughts and words and slipping into your heart and the world of feeling and tone. It is not one of making an intellectual connection as much as it is a feeling connection.

Check in with your heart and ask yourself if all feels well concerning your family. Look at them through the awareness of your heart, one by one. Listen to them with an open heart. Observe their movement, their tone, their energy. Remember that such energy is very subtle, so avoid negating what you feel in expectation of strong feelings. With practice you will pick up on more and more, especially if you are grounded and clearheaded in your own energy.

You can further tune in to someone's personal vibration through consciously noticing all that you can when you are with them—in other words, by noticing what is emanating *from* them, whether it's calm, quiet, agitated, frightened, healthy or sick, strong or weak. You can tune in to your children's personal vibrations through rocking them, massaging their backs, holding their hands, listening to their voices and to their heartbeats. All of those activities we often call "bonding" are really the act of becoming familiar with another's personal vibration.

Because a personal vibration is composed of physical, emotional, and intuitive energy, it can be weakened in any number of ways. Poor health, stress, exhaustion, or poor nutrition will alter a personal vibration. Too much sugar, alcohol, or drugs will weaken for sure. Being upset, angry, afraid, or hysterical will weaken it, as can negative people who drain or frighten us. It is up to a sensitive and heart-based, aware parent to notice and identify a dissonant personal vibration, just as a sensitive musician can identify a "sour note."

SOUR NOTES

Aware mothers and fathers can sense when a child's personal vibration is off balance. Usually it begins as a very subtle shift, and many times parents will choose to ignore it, wanting more concrete proof that something is wrong. If we as parents would stop doubting our wisdom and trust our intuition and perceptions around our children, many problems could be corrected before getting out of hand.

I have a client, Allen, who is the divorced father of a boy and girl. One day his son, Larry, was visiting him and was apparently fine, but, as Allen said, "He seemed off by one shade, and it bothered me." Allen called his ex-wife and queried her. Was Larry okay? Did he seem fine to her? She assured him that Larry was just fine, but Allen wasn't satisfied. He asked Larry many questions about life, his health, his state of mind, and with some prodding got him to admit that he didn't feel great and had been pretty tired lately. He was just covering it up because he didn't want to create more problems between his parents.

Though his ex-wife thought he was being obsessive, Allen followed his heart and insisted that Larry get checked out. The next day he took Larry to the doctor, who found, with testing, that Larry's blood count was abnormal and diagnosed leukemia. Fortunately in Larry's case, thanks to his very alert and intuitive father, he was treated early and is now in remission. Allen often wonders what would have happened had he not noticed and trusted his feelings and pushed the issue with his ex-wife.

Another client, Dylan, also knew her seven-year-old son John's vibration well enough to sense that something was not right with him when he started second grade. An extremely bright kid, even termed gifted by his teachers, Dylan had no reason to worry about him, but in her heart she did. When she voiced her feelings to her husband, he thought she was being a worrywart, but even his criticism and dismissal didn't deter her.

Finally, acting purely on her instinct, she had John tested at a learning center. There they discovered that John had severe dyslexia and gradual hearing loss. The reason it was not immediately apparent was that he had a photographic memory, which he used to compensate for his difficulties. Dylan immediately set about getting him remedial help, and eventually he was fitted with a hearing aid. His problems were diagnosed early enough to avoid more serious setbacks. It was all due to Dylan's intuition and her truly knowing her son's vibration well enough to investigate.

You can protect and help your children if you become sensitive and attuned to their personal vibrations. Whether it is physical distress or intuitive distress, our kids send us signals when they are out of balance that we need to notice.

TRUST WHAT YOU FEEL

Living in the intuitive mode means being as comfortable with the nonphysical dimensions of who we are as with the physical dimensions. It means being able to sense and acknowledge nonphysical vibrations as readily as we acknowledge red lights, green lights, and stop signs. Being aware of your children's personal vibrations will alert you whenever anything is off on any level, but that will not be enough to bring it into balance. It's only when you trust your heart, *respond* to these signals, and act on your instincts that your own intuition will begin to serve you and your children well. Knowing our children's personal vibrations, we as parents can better sense our children's invisible energy fields. Know that we *can* feel them. We simply need to honor these feelings without question. Our children will take their cues from us. If we freely acknowledge our energy fields and listen to our subtle, heart-based, intuitive inclinations regarding them, and say so, so will they. It is so refreshing when that happens! It's calling a spade a spade and allows for the adjustments these personal vibrations occasionally need.

Get to know the personal vibrations of your family members. One child may have a solid, grounded feeling; another may be more ethereal and delicate. A child who is athletic and physically inclined may have a more intense personal vibration than one who is sensitive and artistic. Not that a child can't be artistic and strong, or artistic and grounded; he can. Everyone is unique. It is simply up to you to become familiar with your child's unique energy personality. Your own instincts will guide you. Knowing your child's energy well will alert you when it is off. Always take these instincts seriously and act on them as they arise.

Whether it is noticing their physical well-being, emotional disposition, social orientation, or spiritual integrity, be aware of who your children really are and trust your instincts as if they were the most important thing in the world. In fact, they are.

WHAT ABOUT YOUR OWN PERSONAL VIBRATION?

Just as every other member of your family has a distinct personal vibration, so do you, and when your vibration is disrupted, your sensitivity and perception of everyone else in the family will be compromised, and they will feel it! Conditions such as excessive negativity, anger, extreme stress, sickness, and exhaustion seriously alter one's intuitive perception and throw it out of balance, as do addictions and poor diet. All these conditions interfere with your clarity and ability to be intuitive and tuned in to your family and throw them off balance as well.

Just last week I was working at home on a writing project and feeling terribly pressured. My anxiety spilled over into the atmosphere, and soon enough I could feel my daughter Sabrina reacting to the tension. That day it was my personal vibration that was off. I was sitting at one end of the room, writing, while Sabrina was working on a project of her own at the other end of the room. Neither of us spoke, both of us were deep in concentration, but after fifteen minutes Sabrina stood up.

"That's it, Mom. I have to go downstairs. Your energy is filling up this room with bad feelings, and I can't breathe. I need oxygen!" And she collected her stuff and walked out. On the way out the door she yelled back at me, "You shouldn't work so hard. Your energy is *off*!"

Her point was well taken. I put down my pen, took in a deep breath, and began to laugh. Then I got up and went for a bike ride to rebalance myself. My personal vibration obviously needed a tune-up!

It doesn't matter whose energy is off or who feels it first. It's more important to pay attention to everyone's energy and if someone is off, say so. Then take a few minutes to relax and rebalance.

In addition to affecting the balance of your personal vibration, physical fatigue, emotional strain, and mental exhaustion will play tricks on your ability to be accurately perceptive of anyone's personal vibration, causing one of two consequences. The first is a condition of hypersensitivity, when your intuition goes haywire and you begin picking up everything and anything in the "ethers," so to speak. The psychic equivalent of tuning in to ten radio stations at once, on full volume, it can lead to confusion, overreaction, anxiety attacks, and blowups and prevent you from having a clear, grounded awareness of the energy around you.

A second, opposite effect is to tune out vibrations altogether and shut down or go into tunnel vision, seeing only what you want to see. When this happens you are aware of only part of the scenario and miss the bigger, clearer picture of reality around you, thus distancing yourself from your kids and what the situation really requires. I call this the "rose-colored glasses syndrome." Neither condition is desirable and will compromise your ability to be tuned and aware on a level that can best provide the kind of psychic protection and sensitivity that such heightened awareness can provide.

The way to avoid either condition is to be responsible for yourself and stay mentally healthy and physically grounded. This means knowing when to relax. To exercise. To meditate. It means not overworking as well as avoiding or addressing any addictions you may have. It also means arming yourself with reliable information instead of being run by your fears, as well as keeping a healthy optimism about life and staying in touch with your heart. Basically, it means having a certain common sense that you are a spiritual being in a physical body and that there are requirements for both body and soul in order for you to maintain a clear and perceptive psychic well-being.

Tool MENTAL BREATHERS

One way to keep your personal perception clear, grounded, and tuned in to accurate readings of your family and life all around you is to practice what I call daily "mental breathers." Take one or two daily breaks of five to ten minutes to retreat from whatever you are doing and simply relax into a moment of tranquillity. These mental breaks can center around a cup of tea (not coffee—too much caffeine!), a quick stroll around the block, or simply sitting back and looking out the window. Taking mental breaks during the day will strengthen and tone your own vibration and rebalance any minor dissonance you may have.

Establishing the habit of "mental breaks" will create an inner oasis for you to retreat into whenever you are agitated, annoyed, or worried and enable you to keep your personal vibration clear and grounded. By taking mental breaks regularly, you fortify the inner oasis, which helps you differentiate between true "bad vibes" and simple static or imbalance within yourself.

Tool MAKE A NOTE OF IT

One of the more exciting ways to teach yourself to tune in to personal vibrations is to carry around a little pocket notebook or tape recorder. Every time you feel any little hint, twinge, vibe, or subtle notion regarding a child or family member, rather than mulling it over and wondering whether or not it is valid, simply notice the "vibe" and write it down or record it. For example, you might write: "Anna was very nervous and subdued after school today—I wonder if something or someone upset her." Or you may write: "I've been thinking of Phil all day. I wonder if everything is all right on his trip to visit his father." Writing down or recording these feelings will accomplish several important things. First, it tells your subconscious mind that you now intend to notice and value your "vibes." Second, it frees you from the temptation to ignore such feelings.

A client, Marianne, tried this tool with her own kids. At first she said she felt as though she were almost making up feelings just to have something to write down. But after a week of practicing this tool, she had an overwhelming feeling that her sixteen-year-old daughter, Ida, who was on her first solo camping trip with her two girlfriends, was in trouble. After she had recorded her impression the feeling only got stronger—so strong, in fact, that she felt compelled to get in the car and go to the campsite where she knew they'd be. Feeling silly, she nevertheless followed her hunch. When she arrived at the campsite she discovered Ida along with her friends huddled around their car, attempting to fix a flat tire in the dark. The minute Ida saw her mom pull up, she screamed for joy. They didn't have a clue as to what they were doing, and what should have been a relatively simple task had turned into a monumental disaster. Ida was particularly worried that they might be stranded, and even though the situation wasn't dire, it was emotionally scary for the girls to be in such a bind in the middle of nowhere at night. All three girls were thrilled to see help arrive. "Mom, I kept sending you vibes to help us," Ida said. "I can't believe you actually got them!"

Writing down your perceptions clears the mind and sharpens awareness, and if done regularly, it will provide you with feedback on the importance of what you are noticing.

Tool SPEAK UP

Talk about any personal vibrations you may have with your family, and encourage them to do the same. Doing this will demonstrate to your children that in your home the subtle, nonphysical realm of energy is acknowledged as much as the physical plane.

In our family we tune in to one another's personal vibration by openly expressing our vibes when we have them. For example, one day I had a vibe that something was off with Sonia, and I asked her if anything was out of balance. At first she said, "I'm fine," but after a few minutes she reconsidered. "I'm not really fine. I'm having trouble with French, and I feel like the other kids in my class think I'm dumb." Then she burst into tears. Once my feeling was confirmed, Patrick and I began to give her a lot more support, and in no time she had found her confidence once again.

Sharing personal vibes helps us tune in to our hearts, clears the air, and keeps everyone's awareness crisp, keen, and sharp, the perfect condition for activating intuition. After doing this exercise for a while, we have found that we have fine-tuned our sensitivity to one another to a very caring and gentle level. It keeps us conscious of how vulnerable we all are and prevents us from falling into an unconscious rut. It also keeps our awareness unclogged and our hearts open to inspiration.

FALSE ALARMS VERSUS REAL PROBLEMS

Inevitably the highest priority for the family is the safety and protection of the children. A true familiarity with your kids' personal vibrations will help.

"But how do I know if I'm tuning in to true problems around my kids or if I'm just getting worked up over nothing?" asked one eager but anxious mother. "I often worry about my son, especially when he's traveling by plane. If I'm not careful, I go into a full-blown anxiety attack until he's landed safely. Is that a true vibe or a false alarm?"

This is a good question, and probably more important than any other for parents. If you are a parent to whom this sort of thing often happens (and it happens to nearly *all* parents at one time or another), it is important to know that the source of the anxiety you are feeling *is* psychic in nature but doesn't necessarily mean the disaster you fear.

What actually happens at these anxious times is that the intuitive connection you have with your child gets temporarily disconnected, much as a radio can temporarily lose a particular station signal owing to interference. This disconnection can happen because of worry, confusion, or sometimes even the child's own desire for freedom and independence, especially if you are an overly controlling or domineering parent. It's the psychic "disconnect" itself that alarms you and usually not an outside threat or premonition. The fact that you can't feel your child's energy at all is what causes your concern and the tendency to go into all kinds of worst-case scenario imaginings. Most likely your child is just fine, but when you do experience such psychic disruptions, there is something you can do besides work yourself into a nervous wreck:

Tool RENEWING CONNECTIONS

> If you feel disconnected from your child, simply
> focus on your heart and think of your child. Say
> your child's name to yourself and ask Divine Spirit
> to surround that child with a pure white light of
> loving protection. Imagine this white light com-
> pletely covering your child and whoever he might be
> with or come into contact with, wherever they are.
> See your child in your mind's eye as safe, protected,
> and in total peace. And while you're at it, send your
> child your love.

This visualization will help you reconnect with your children's vibration
and hold them in safety wherever they are. You will be doing something
energetically to balance your vibration and theirs and reestablish the
connection you share.

"But what if you are feeling something bad, and no visualization in
the world will help?" asked another anxious mom. If you have bad
vibes about your children and cannot calm down, and have no way of
contacting your family, then I suggest that you pray for their protection.
It is all you can do. Even though it would be terrific to circumvent or
control every single potential problem that your children will ever
encounter by using your intuition, that would be more than any human
being can possibly do or even expect of himself. That is God's work.
Calming your energy and sending loving and protective energy to the
ones you love most does help enormously, whatever the circumstances.
If you are picking up vibes that are so strong that you can't relax unless
you do something about it, then I suggest that you try to inform those
involved if possible and do what I suggested in chapter 1. Ask your family to respect your feelings and change their plans or keep in touch and
reassure you, even if only to "humor you." Hopefully, they will. That
way, no matter what you are sensing, true vibe or false alarm, "all bases
are covered," so to speak, in terms of protecting your family and staying
calm and grounded yourself.

ENERGY IN MOTION

As you begin to tune in to the world of energy, there are times when your vibes will confuse you. For example, you may have a worrisome feeling about your child, yet it turns out that everything is just fine. Does that mean your intuition isn't reliable?

Not necessarily. When it comes to intuition, being "right" shouldn't be your absolute goal, especially when you are just beginning to become more sensitive to energy. Accurately picking up on energy is a refined skill that develops with lots of practice and lots of errors if you are to become good at it. Besides, if you pick up troubling vibes, yet nothing seems amiss, don't be so sure you were off. You may be tuning in to a precarious moment where real danger or imbalance does exist, but the situation may correct itself somehow before it evolves into a real or more serious problem. After all, energy, and life, is not fixed, but always in a state of motion.

A client of mine told me about this experience with her daughter. Janice, the very intuitive and aware mother of a seventeen-year-old daughter named Lisa, offered to chaperone Lisa and her girlfriends on a spring break trip to Cancún. Wanting to give her daughter "space" while still being present, Janice stayed in a separate room during the five days they would be there.

One morning Lisa told her mother that she and her friends were going to the beach, and they agreed to meet at five for dinner. All day long Janice had a terrible feeling around her daughter's vibration. She felt that her daughter was not okay. This feeling fluctuated from mild worry to moments of real psychic upset. "What's going on with Lisa?" she asked herself, certain something was off. She surrounded Lisa with white light, and gradually the anxiety passed.

Finally five rolled around and Janice called her daughter's room. "Lisa's in the shower," said Chris, one of Lisa's roommates. "Hold on, I'll see if she's out."

While she was waiting, Janice could hear the girls talking, and she overheard Chris say, "Thank God I stopped Lisa from having sex on the beach today!"

Janice almost dropped the phone. No wonder I was so upset! she thought. What was Lisa thinking? What were the girls up to?

A moment later Lisa picked up the phone. "Hi, Mom!" she said, sounding like her usual cheerful self.

"Lisa," Janice said, containing her righteous indignation and alarm, "I need to talk to you! Please come up to my room right now."

Lisa strolled into Janice's room a few minutes later and sat down. Unable to restrain herself any longer, Janice blurted out, "Lisa, I overheard Chris say that she stopped you from having sex on the beach! Now what on earth were you doing?"

Lisa was surprised and puzzled. "I don't know what you're talking about, Mom. For that matter, how could you even think I'd do anything so ridiculous as that!"

"Lisa, I had terrible vibes about you all afternoon. There's no point in trying to cover up. I felt you were up to something myself!"

Lisa seemed confused for a moment and then burst out laughing.

"I'm sorry, Mom! I just figured it out! Sex on the Beach is the name of the tequila shooters they were selling at the beach bar, and I was thinking of trying one."

Greatly relieved, Janice had to laugh, too.

Were Janice's vibes off? I don't think so. A seventeen-year-old girl should not be drinking tequila shooters, much less in a foreign country! Did Janice's prayers and visualizations help? Well, Lisa never did have Sex on the Beach.

Picking up vibrations is not about whether they turn out to be "right or wrong." It's about tuning in to energy in motion and keeping it balanced. Our energy isn't static. It's fluid, mobile, and alive, changing with the circumstances. Lisa was temporarily in a position to cause damage to herself, which Janice accurately tuned in to. But perhaps it was Janice's prayers themselves that actually turned the situation around and restored balance. I believe it was.

Tuning in to a personal vibration is a skill involving awareness, sensitivity, and groundedness. It centers in the heart and connects you to your children, and with practice it can become as natural as breathing. The ability to accurately notice your child's personal vibration, and especially to recognize any imbalances or threats to this energy, takes a clear, centered awareness on your part. Taking mental breathers, practicing meditation, keeping yourself in physical and emotional balance, maintaining a clear and grounded home, and taking the time to bond with your children are the essential keys to keeping this connection strong, intact, and uninterrupted. This clear connection is the lifeline to the intuitive life you share.

Tool ENERGY EXCHANGE

While breathing gently, put one hand on your heart and one hand on your child's heart. Now, with eyes closed, mentally notice the child's energy and ask your heart to notify you of any dissonance, physically, emotionally, or mentally. Do not be overly analytical during this exercise. Simply relax and accept whatever comes up. Then open your eyes and share your feelings, if the child is old enough. If not, write them into your notebook.

You can also do this from a distance, through visualizing that you are placing your hand on your child's heart. This is also an exercise that you can teach children to do, and it is one they love to practice and can use their entire lives.

Tool UP CLOSE AND PERSONAL

When you are with your child, close your eyes for a moment and with full awareness pay attention to how it feels physically to be close to her, to hug her, to hear and feel her breath near you. Breathe in as you do this.

Then do the same exercise with your eyes open.

Tool HAND IT OVER

Tell your child you want to spend a few special moments together. Suggest that you not talk during this time. Give your child a hand or foot massage for five minutes. Simply focus your awareness on your child's body and notice how your energy affects your child. Remember to breathe. Notice whether or not your child feels calm or restless as you work. Notice whether your child feels healthy and vibrant or wimpy and weak. Is your child open to receiving energy, or is he blocking your attention? Do you notice anything else? Ask your child how he feels when receiving a massage from you.

Have your child do the same for you.

Tool HEALING YOUR VIBRATION

Begin by quieting your own personal vibration with a few deep, relaxing breaths. Next, focus your full attention on the center of your heart and acknowledge three things that you love about yourself. Be fair, generous, and gentle. As you acknowledge your lovable qualities, feel this flow of self-love and acceptance moving throughout your entire energy field. Next, gently call the name of your child and visualize placing her in the center of your heart.

Now send this same flow of self-love and acceptance to your child. Imagine this loving energy beginning in the center of your child's heart and flowing outward, filling up her entire being with love and acceptance. See your child completely engulfed in your love—appreciating, healing, calming, and balancing your child's vibration. Do this for two or three minutes. When you are finished, open your eyes.

Tool SEVEN WAYS TO CHECK IN

1. Look into your child's eyes for two minutes without speaking and send love.

2. Wake your child up *gently* in the morning, and send love.

3. Tuck your child into bed with a leisurely good night, and send love.

4. Look into your child's eyes and say, "I love you," and then send love.

5. Notice how your child moves, speaks, sits, talks, plays. Pay attention to any subtle shifts. Ask your heart for guidance in noticing when anything is off balance.

6. Put a white loving light of protection around your child every day.

7. Put a white loving light around yourself, too.

Reflections

1. Practice paying attention to each family member's personal vibration. Can you describe it in any way? Yours?

_____

_____

_____

Your spouse's or partner's?

_____

_____

_____

Your first child's?

_____

_____

_____

Your second child's?

_____

_____

_____

Your third child's?

_____

_____

_____

Your fourth child's?

_____

_____

_____

2. Are you able to identify when your family member's personal vibrations are off? Yours?

_____

_____

_____

3. Do you acknowledge it? What do you do about it?

_____

_____

_____

4. Do you have any special bonding habits with your family that help you connect with their personal vibrations?

_____

_____

_____

5. Are you taking care of your mental, physical, and emotional health and well-being so that you are able to clearly tune in to personal vibrations?

_____

_____

_____

6. In becoming more aware of personal vibrations, are you noticing any more about your family? Your partner? Yourself?

_____

_____

_____

7. Have you had any intuitive insights regarding any of you? What are they?

_____

_____

_____

REMINDERS
Are you:
    Tuning in to your heart?
    Simplifying your schedule?
    Keeping your house clutter free and serene?
    Noticing subtle vibrations and tuning in to vibes?

SPECIAL NOTE
Another way to bring a personal vibration back into balance is with many types of flower remedies. There are flower essences designed specifically to restore harmony and balance in the case of emotional or intuitive dissonance. Flower essences and information on their benefits can be found in most health food stores. If you can't find them, go to your local library and look in the subject catalog under "flower remedies."

These remedies can help restore psychic and emotional balance, but they do not take the place of basic health care, good food, and an emotionally healthy atmosphere. Yet they are wonderful supplements and can bring about great shifts in one's personal vibration. Check them out for yourself!

SIX

The Language of Spirit

One of my psychic mentors, Charlie Goodman, taught me some-thing very important about awakening intuition. He said that the decision not only to feel an intuition but actually to *express* that intuition makes all the difference in the world.

"Being aware of an intuition is only part of the process," he would say. "Putting that feeling into expression in the world is the other part. When you do that you put value on it, and when you put value on your intuition it can then begin to help you in life."

Because so many people do not come from a family background where intuition was acknowledged, they often feel awkward or uncomfortable in openly expressing intuitive feelings. To a large degree this may be due simply to the fact that they do not have a language that allows them to express their intuition comfortably and without self-consciousness.

Some people, when they do express their feelings, call them "a weird feeling," or a "funny," "bizarre," "creepy," or "scary" feeling. The problem with these terms is that their connotation is negative, and intuitive feelings then become associated with something unpleasant. If you say, for example, that you had a weird experience, many people will automatically look at you as if *you* are weird, no matter what the experience was. And as most parents know, no child wants to be thought of as weird! Children are very sensitive to how they are perceived by other kids. If they are perceived this way, they suffer. They would rather ignore their intuition, and they do.

Another, more cavalier attempt to describe intuitive life is to call such events "odd experiences" or "strange coincidences." These terms allow acknowledgment of intuitive experiences but cast them as flukes, as aberrations from the norm, certainly nothing to be recognized as significant.

Probably the best phrases for expressing intuitive feelings are those that are organically based—"I have a gut feeling," "a tight chest," "a lump in my throat," "butterflies in my stomach." These expressions focus on where the intuitive energy being picked up is felt in the body. But they, too, often fall short of being taken seriously.

In our family intuition was so fundamental to our way of life that we actually had code words for the very purpose of acknowledging and expressing our intuition, words that were quite specific and yet conveyed complex feelings. This language made it easy for us to share what we felt, bypassing the intellectual and emotional barriers explanations set up. The very fact that there were words we could use for various intuitive flashes was justification in itself that those feelings were valid and worth noticing.

The first of our code words was "vibes," meaning the initial energy sensation of intuition in the body. Vibes were broken down into categories. We had "good vibes," meaning all people, places, ideas, and possibilities that evoked positive, safe, happy sensations. Good vibes indicated a "green light, go for it" type of decision and described synchronicities, beneficial encounters, and sensations of protection and grace.

We also had "bad vibes," meaning all uncomfortable, uneasy, unsafe feelings. Bad vibes were those cautious "stay away, don't do it, don't trust it, watch out, be careful, keep on your toes" instincts that alerted us that something was not okay.

We also had other words to describe intuitive states, like "grounded" to describe the sensation of being present, solid, and secure and feeling strong and committed. Then there was "ungrounded," a word to describe a state of being rushed, overwhelmed, overloaded, disconnected, out of harmony with our surroundings, uncomfortable, ill at ease, nervous, defensive, irritable, and vulnerable.

You can see how many subtle states just these two words encompass, and you can understand what a relief it was to us to be able to express all that so simply. We gave no more thought to having bad vibes than we did to seeing a red car. It was just another part of our sensory landscape. Growing up with such basic vocabulary to express intuition has made it extremely easy to integrate my intuition into my adult life as just another everyday, matter-of-fact aspect of my sensory awareness.

SIMPLE WORDS, PROTECTIVE MEASURES

I have continued this tradition of "speaking the language of intuition" with my husband and our children. I have introduced them to these terms that are so familiar to me, and together we have invented others.

Sonia made up the term "woolies" to express the feeling of someone or something that disrupts her inner harmony or equilibrium. It describes conditions or people who have an irritating effect on her, like wool on bare skin. When Sonia says someone "gives her the woolies" I know she feels uncomfortable around them. This was good to know when she was younger and was invited to many of her classmates' birthday parties. If she was asked to attend the party of a "wooly," she simply begged off, knowing she wouldn't like it. It kept her from enduring an unpleasant experience or having to explain to us *why* she didn't want to go. The fact that she felt someone was a "wooly" was explanation enough.

Another term we use in our home is "wide open." This means that we are taking in more stimulation than feels comfortable, and it is causing us to become "ungrounded." In an adult world, being wide open can be felt when you are unexpectedly called into the boss's office only to be criticized or, worse yet, let go. Or you pick up the phone only to have someone "let you have it." You know the feeling. It's the feeling of being overwhelmed, caught off guard, and taken by surprise.

Another term we share is "shut down." Shutting down is similar to closing the windows in a house, a protective measure to push out unwanted influences. I was with Sonia at the airport one day, checking bags, when the man in front of us was throwing a fit at the counter. He was causing such a scene over his reservation mix-up that he had succeeded in getting three ticket agents involved, and now they were beginning to argue among themselves. Their agitation was spilling over to the crowd of waiting passengers, and comments were beginning to fly out for him to "shut up" and "move on." It was an ugly situation and getting worse.

Without a second thought Sonia turned to me and said, "Uh-oh, trouble. Better shut down and ignore it." And she was right. Otherwise we, like the other people around us, would have absorbed the tension.

Another expression that my kids appreciate and that we use to describe unpleasant energy is an "ick attack," a phrase that is instantly recognizable. It's the feeling you get when you are around someone or something that leaves you feeling very disgusted or "icky."

I remember when I was a ninth-grader in Catholic school getting a major ick attack every time I was around the girls' volleyball coach. All the girls loved him, and he seemed nice enough on the surface, but every time I was around him he made me feel "icky," invaded in some way, so I avoided him outside class at all costs. And in tenth grade, when my friend Gina confessed to me that she had been having sex with him for over a year, I was disgusted but not surprised. No wonder he had given me such an ick attack! He was nothing more than a pervert, a slimy, icky one.

The last code word I have been introduced to and have shared with my children is "psychic attack." A psychic attack is stronger than an ick attack, because an ick attack means something or someone is unpleasant or unhealthy, whereas a psychic attack is when someone or something actually wants to hurt you. Psychic attacks occur all the time. It's the ambush from the co-worker who wants your job, or the flaky friend who blames you for his mistake. It's the malicious neighbor who competes with you, or the alcoholic in a rage. Psychic attack is a term to describe the mean-spirited, negative behavior of someone directed against you. A psychic attack is very hurtful, and it is important to arm your children with the ability to recognize the attack for what it is and move away from it when it occurs.

It may not be obvious, but psychic attack occurs all the time with children, and especially with teenagers, because of their insecurities and lack of power. A psychic attack feels like an assault, a wound, or an injury. It's harmful not only because it hurts, but because it causes doubt. It's a very real arrow of negative thought thrown your way, and it can have lasting consequences.

Teaching children about psychic attack will help them move out of harm's way and away from negative energy instead of doing what so many people, especially children, do—internalizing the negativity as shame. When a psychic attack occurs, children will feel hurt and may not know what hit them. But something *has* happened: negative energy has burned right into their own energy field. So many children experience these intuitive injuries and don't know what to do. It causes them to shut down, withdraw, and feel insecure. They need to be taught to recognize when this is happening to them and talk to you about it. In the next chapter I will discuss what you can do to restore balance when a child experiences a psychic attack.

RESPOND WHEN INTUITION SPEAKS

These simple expressions convey huge messages to children. They convey "I understand," "I believe you," "I feel it, too," "I recognize this energy as real"—and last but not least, "Let's take action to protect ourselves and respond to this information."

For example, last year on the Fourth of July all the families on our block closed off the street to have a block party, an annual tradition. The kids ran around, rode bikes, and played games all day, and in the evening we shared a potluck dinner. At dusk a few parents brought out fireworks, and parents and kids alike sat around to watch them.

After about thirty minutes of blasts and kabooms, Sabrina approached me and whispered, "Mom, for some reason I'm scared. There's too much excitement for me. I feel uncomfortable, and I have bad vibes. I'm too wide open. I don't like it."

Sonia, on the other hand, was loving it and wanted to carry on. She is much more naturally grounded than Sabrina is, and the wild energy wasn't affecting her as much. When I checked with her about her vibes, she too said she felt the energy, but not enough to leave the show. Sabrina wanted to go home, which was fine with me. She needed to say no more. We went into the house, but not before alerting Patrick, who was standing some distance away, to how the girls felt. Patrick decided to move the kids back another fifteen feet from the fireworks just to play it safe and to keep Sonia close to him.

Moments later, from inside the house, Sabrina and I heard a flurry of explosions and screams. Seconds later Sonia rushed into the house out of breath.

"You should've seen what just happened!"

Patrick was behind her, looking shaken. "Those bad vibes you had were right on target, Sabrina! When Joe set off the Turbo Man [the granddad finale of the fireworks], it tipped onto its side and fired straight into the crowd! No one was hurt, but it was too close for comfort. We just averted a disaster and decided that was enough for one night."

Sabrina said, "I'm glad I wasn't there."

We all went to bed that night very relieved.

Having words and expressions like "vibes," "grounded," "wide open," or "shut down" gives kids a great way to express what they are intuitively feeling without having to justify their feelings.

YOUR WORDS ARE THE RIGHT WORDS

Because of my work as a professional intuitive, my children have learned from the beginning about subtle levels of psychic and intuitive energy and ways to talk about them. It is not at all unusual to talk with them about not only vibes, ick attacks, and so forth, but also about energy fields, auras, chakras, and other very sophisticated concepts. Though this works well for my family, it is *not* at all essential to use this vocabulary in order to tap into this wonderful inner voice of spirit. You may prefer religious words such as "my angel" or even just "spirit" when talking about vibes. Or you may want to use easy and obvious phrases such as "my gut," "my hunch," or "my feeling." One family I know calls a psychic attack "a stink bomb." Another calls an "ick attack" a "yucky feeling." Yet another calls vibes "radar." The point is that you can invent your own language of spirit. Whatever words *feel* right to you *are* right for you.

Giving children a way to identify and express their intuitive experiences will help them integrate these experiences more comfortably into their lives. It's just so much easier for children to pay attention and respond to intuition if they don't have to *explain* what they feel or, worse, why. If they learn to just feel it, report it, and have their feelings respected, they will communicate.

KNOW WHEN TO KEEP A SECRET

While intuitive and psychic feelings are natural, some people have a long way to go toward a balanced understanding of their intuitive nature. Though the world is changing, misperceptions are still everywhere and can and do shut down a child's spontaneous expression of intuitive feelings. My mother, being savvy to the potential negative reactions we children could have faced from unenlightened others, advised us to keep our code language a secret from disbelieving ears. She explained that people are either open-minded about intuitive and psychic feelings or they aren't, and it was a waste of energy to talk about things such as vibes with people who weren't receptive.

"It's like speaking Greek to somebody who doesn't understand it. Why waste the time? Better to save it for those who do."

It was good advice when I was a child and spared me disparaging remarks from those who were not "tuned in," and I have shared the same advice with my own kids. Perhaps you too may want to suggest to your children that they keep their expressions for intuitive experiences a secret from those who might be inclined to make fun of them or give them a hard time about being intuitive or psychic. Clue your children into the fact that some people may not be as receptive to vibes as they are. They might have a skeptical and insensitive teacher, for example, or more likely make friends with another child who hasn't been introduced to the world of intuitive and psychic energy.

On the other hand, it is a good idea to find others who do speak your language. Growing up, I remember my mom talking to her best friends, Charlotte and Marilyn, also World War II brides from Europe, about vibes all the time. It was nothing unusual for them to share their psychic experiences or to call one another and ask about their intuitive feeling on matters. They were each other's support system, and having each other to talk to made it much easier for them to listen to their intuition. Following their example, I also had two friends, Sue and Vickie, whom I shared my vibes with as a kid. One of our favorite games in junior high was I Am Psychic, in which we used to predict things, such as who liked whom in the class, or who would win the cheerleading championship, or what teacher was going to "pop" a quiz on us, using all sorts of code words, sign language, and signals. These little exercises in intuition helped shore up our shaky preadolescent self-images, and we had terrific fun testing our skills. Having psychic adventures with friends was the best fun, and we were constantly amazing each other by how accurate we became with each other's encouragement. I'm certain they helped influence my love of intuitive exploration to this day.

BODY LANGUAGE: THE MOST DIRECT

In addition to the language of words, our family has one more code system that allows my children to convey their vibes freely and without fear—body language. We have agreed that in any situation, any one of us may take another's hand and with a series of squeezes convey several feelings. For example, if either Sonia or Sabrina is nervous, one squeeze of the hand means "I'm ungrounded, protect me." Two squeezes means "Bad vibes, I don't like it, let's go!" And one long hand squeeze means "Good vibes, I *do* like it." This silent connection allows us to touch base with one another and our feelings in an even more profound way than words will allow.

For boys who are not hand holders, a few shoulder squeezes or arm taps can do the same thing. As a family you can invent your own code, whether in words or body language. The important thing is to set up a system of communicating your intuitive vibes freely and *privately*.

CREATING YOUR FAMILY'S LANGUAGE OF SPIRIT

Creating a language of spirit provides a framework to help your child express intuition without fear of censorship, to give it the value it deserves, and to receive the benefits that it brings. It allows you and your children to get around the tendency, born out of bad habits, to dismiss the idea that intuition is not real and not available to us.

Intuition is a natural part of who we are, and having a comfortable creative vocabulary to express it will help us reclaim it as part of our lives.

Tool CREATE YOUR OWN LANGUAGE

Ask each family member to describe their intuition using their own code words. Together, have fun building an intuition vocabulary that is all encompassing and supportive to your inner guidance. (If someone in your family is disinterested, don't worry about it. Curiosity usually will engage even the most skeptical, especially if the rest of the family is having fun with this tool.)

_____   _____

_____   _____

_____   _____

_____   _____

_____   _____

_____   _____

Tool WHAT LANGUAGE DO THEY SPEAK?

As a family, notice the descriptive words and phrases that other people use to express intuition, then talk about these expressions at home.

Tool SECRET AGENT

As a family, agree on several code signals to express intuition nonverbally to one another. Ask each family member for his or her input in creating a secret language that will protect and support everyone.

_____

_____

_____

Reflections

1. Write down your family's favorite expressions for:
   An intuition

_____

_____

_____

A good intuition

_____

_____

_____

A bad intuition

_____

_____

_____

2. Write down your family's words for:
Feeling energetically uncomfortable

_____

_____

A psychic attack

_____

_____

The "woolies"

_____

_____

An "ick attack"

_____

_____

Any others

_____

_____

_____

3. Did your family of origin have code words to express their intuition? What were they?

_____

_____

_____

4. Could you speak freely about your intuition as a child? Who listened to you, and how did they respond?

_____

_____

_____

5. Do you speak freely about your intuition today? With whom?

_____

_____

_____

6. Do your children speak freely about their intuition? With whom?

_____

_____

_____

7. Does your partner or spouse speak freely with you about their intuition? How do you respond?

_____

_____

_____

8. Do your extended family members, parents, siblings, share their intuitive feelings freely? What expressions do they use?

_____

_____

_____

9. Do your family members use validating words to describe intuition? Or is their language colored with discomfort or confusion or invalidation of their intuition?

_____

_____

_____

10. Have you noticed any difference in your intuition since introducing a language of spirit?

_____

_____

_____

REMINDERS
Are you:
    Simplifying your schedule?
    Keeping your house clutter free and serene?
    Noticing subtle vibrations?
    Creating your own language of spirit?

✳ SEVEN

Building Boundaries

As you continue to accept intuition as a natural part of your spiritual nature, you will quickly burst into a whole new dimension of awareness. You will discover that awakening intuition is like noticing stars. For the longest time you can go along never noticing the night sky overhead. Then one night you look up and notice sparkling stars in the sky. Taken by their lovely twinkle, you become drawn into the blackness, seeking more bright sky lights. At first you may see only a few, then more, then still more, until quite spontaneously your whole perception shifts and suddenly the skies seem to explode with thousands upon thousands of stars. It's humbling to realize that although these lights were in the sky all along, you are noticing them for the first time.

As you begin to tune in to the realm of spirit, intuition begins to sparkle like stars in the night sky. Once your perceptions are set to notice intuition, suddenly a surge of synchronicity and "ah-hah!"

moments of psychic perception begins to flow like water. One of the ways you will notice intuition more and more is that you and your family will begin to perceive the energy fields of the people around you, and the more you know about these fields, the better you will be able to respond to them.

One day as I was putting Sonia to bed she said, "Mom, do you know people glow?"

"What do you mean?" I asked.

"I saw Bobby get really mad at Susan in school today, and when he was screaming at her, just over his head I saw a glowing red light. For real!" She burst out laughing.

"You saw Bobby's aura, Sonia. It's the energy field that surrounds his body," I explained. "We all have an aura or energy field. It surrounds our bodies, and sometimes it can even absorb energy from others like a sponge. When a person is angry, as Bobby was, their energy field turns red. That's why people sometimes say, 'I was so mad I was seeing red.' They are."

I continued to explain to Sonia that this energy field has many names. Another name for an energy field is the etheric body. Etheric stems from the word "ether," meaning spirit. An aura or etheric body is your spirit body. It follows the outline of your physical body, extending from one to five feet outward from it. A sensitive, intuitive person can sometimes see this field, as Sonia did that morning. But even when you don't *see* it, it can still be felt, and it does affect us.

A RAINBOW OF POSSIBILITY

This energy field can change in tone and color depending upon how a person feels, physically, mentally, and emotionally. When someone is passionate, angry, or even frightened, the energy field will glow red and feel intense, brittle, and agitated. If a person is frightened, tired, or physically ill, this red can change to a muddy brown, and that person will feel sticky, drained, and sluggish. When a person is excited, delighted, feeling creative, or sensing pleasure, her aura will become bright orange and feel vibrant, energized, and alive. When someone is deep in thought, concentrating, focusing, or trying to take control of things, his aura will turn bright yellow and feel intense, sharp, and dynamic. When a person feels loved or loving, or is at peace with her surroundings, her aura will become bright green and will feel engaging, warm, and healing. When someone feels kindness, affection, even romance, the green will become flecked with pink tones and will feel safe, calming, and compelling.

If a person is listening to his heart, or if he is in a state of receptivity, as when he is learning and sharing ideas, his aura will become sky blue and feel lucid, clear, and inspiring. If a person has an active imagination, or is a visual thinker, that person's energy field will turn a deep indigo blue and feel adventurous, deep, and insightful. If a person is in a state of prayer, meditation, or contemplation or is feeling the love and guidance of the Universe, her aura will become violet white, sometimes flecked with gold, and will feel soothing, profound, even sacred.

These changes in color in the energy field reflect one's vitality, frame of mind, perspective, emotions, and physical condition. Therefore, since people, including children, have complex makeups, these energy fields are usually a blend of colors and influences. When we are relaxed and conscious of energy beyond just the physical dimension, we can feel and sometimes see these energy fields.

INSIGHT OVER EYESIGHT

Sonia's seeing Bobby's energy field was no big deal. I think all children see auras at one time or another, usually when they are very young. Their eyes are attuned to this frequency of vibration because their minds are clear and their hearts are open. They are so much more aware of their energetic surroundings than we adults, who spend much of our time filtering out information because our minds are preoccupied with past or future events.

Sue, a client of mine who had adopted two children, made an appointment with me to discuss her four-year-old daughter, Linda, who talked about the colors surrounding every member of the family. "At times she tells me she sees a yellow light around her brother's head," she said. "And once she mentioned that she saw a pink light around my face. I know she's seeing our auras, but I'm not exactly sure how to explain that to her."

I suggested that she simply explain to her daughter that she was tuning in to energy fields. "I think you may be surprised at how readily Linda will accept your explanation. Just tell her that the energy she is seeing surrounds everyone's bodies, and that she is lucky that she can see it."

Sue did just that, to which Linda responded, "So that's what you call that light!"

I believe all children start out seeing auras as babies. Some, like Linda, retain the ability for longer than others, but most lose this ability by the age of three or four. By then their perspective has been influenced, causing them to focus *away* from more subtle energy planes and focus exclusively on the physical universe.

SENSING THE AURA

Even if children stop seeing auras, they do not stop *feeling* or reacting to them, and with a little effort in awareness, neither do adults. Our auric fields are the sum total of our consciousness and personal vibration at any given time, and children can and do feel this consciousness quite acutely.

If we are tense or angry, our auric field will convey that just as our personal vibration does. If we are weak or tired, joyous or happy, scared or courageous, our energy will all be conveyed in an auric field. As we come into contact with energy fields surrounding other people, we are affected by them, and we can even absorb another's energy. This is good if we are around a positive vibration, but if we aren't careful, we can also be affected by negative energy.

Can you ever recall being around someone so surly or unpleasant that you felt their energy crawling all over you like bugs? Or draining you so much that you needed a nap? Remember how, once you got away from the person, you could still feel the agitated energy as though that person were still around? So much so that you became just as agitated as he was? That's because that person's energy field—his aura—

contaminated your own. Did you ever wake up on the wrong side of the bed and feel like a dishrag before you even shuffled to breakfast? Weren't you ever amazed at how you caused the whole family to get uptight without even saying good morning? In that case it's your auric field that is contaminating the room.

On the other hand, have you ever been around a loving, sweet person, such as a six-month-old baby in a good mood? Are you aware of how this loving and open heart immediately lightens your own, leaving you feeling cheered and happy inside? Or have you ever seen the look of a child watching a parade? The wonder and delight radiated is contagious.

The reason for this is that human beings seek harmony and resonance with their environment. If there is a dominant vibration in our space, we unconsciously tune in to it. For example, if you put two guitars side by side and pluck a string on one of them, the same string will vibrate on the other. This is called the law of resonance. We are like those guitars, only more so. We also feel and resonate with other people's energy fields all the time, only most people are usually unconscious about this phenomenon. Therefore, when around calm energy we become calm, and when around upset energy we can easily fall into feeling this upset ourselves.

As you can see, energy fields are real, and they readily affect us, especially kids. Have you ever noticed how quickly kids react to someone who is being uptight? They can't stand it. They will act out or be rude or do something impolite or withdraw because the anxious person's energy makes them uncomfortable.

Or how about the aura power of Mom? In our house, if my mother was unhappy, you could feel it seeping out from under the front door before you even opened it. She only had to walk into a room, and if something was out of order, her energy had us all in her grip. In our house the saying "happy mom, happy family" was the national anthem. Her energy was so powerful that we all felt what she felt, so of course we wanted her to feel happy. I wonder if everyone's mom's aura had the same effect ours did. After talking to clients for years, I think so.

Perceiving auric energy and learning how to either dodge it or try to improve it is how children who grow up in homes with violence, alcoholism, and generally destructive vibrations manage to survive, even though they don't know they're doing this. The more sensitive children will languish and can become very withdrawn and sick if the energy around them is extremely negative. But those children who don't languish manage to survive by shutting down their hearts completely and tuning out their responsiveness to others. The problem is that it's hard to tune out vibrations when you feel them—so hard, in fact, that kids sometimes resort to extreme measures to do so. They reach for drugs, alcohol, even food. These substances override their awareness and shut down sensitivity, temporarily dulling the pain of disturbed family vibrations. Addiction is a sorry solution, but it serves a purpose. Unfortunately it also shuts down consciousness, self-esteem, empathy, creativity, and joy.

We need to pay close attention to *how* others' energy affects us so that we can take steps to prevent them from affecting us negatively. So often a child is exposed to another person's unpleasant or negative energy, only to be shushed or ignored by the parent or authority at hand. Sometimes it is even the parent himself who is giving off the toxic energy. If kids are silenced or ignored or if negative energy is inflicted upon them often enough, they will begin to doubt their experience and shut down their awareness.

AURA INVASION

A client, Dawn, told me this story about her daughter, Sharon. One year Sharon befriended a little girl at camp who had a very unsettled aura. She was competitive and jealous, and though Sharon played with her, it was mostly because she was too accommodating to object to the other girl's treatment of her. Every day Sharon would come home from camp with an aura filled with tension and abuse from her experience with the new girl. She sucked it in all day, taking the barbs, jabs, and manipulation while keeping her mouth shut and perhaps not fully understanding what was happening. As soon as she was home, where it was safe, she'd spew out this toxic energy, making a terrible scene. She'd cry, or whine, or start a fight with her younger brother. In fact, she'd behave with the same poor manners and disrespect that she had endured all day long. This went on for a month.

One day Dawn called and asked me for advice. I suggested to her that she help Sharon understand that she had picked up negative energy from the other child and that she needed to clear it.

Sharon, looking both intrigued and somewhat relieved that her mother noticed that she needed help, responded enthusiastically. "How do we clear energy, Mom?" she asked. Dawn then shared what she had learned from me.

"Cleaning your aura is easy," she said, "and it's something to do when you've been around negativity, rudeness, abuse, or any energy that you simply don't like."

"In that case, Mom, I have to clean it every day, because there's always someone bothering me at camp," Sharon said. Here is how they did it.

Tool HOUSE CLEANING

First, go outside. (If weather doesn't permit, go into a quiet room.) Stamp your feet or, better yet, jump up and down a few times and draw in a deep, clear breath. Next, rub your hands over your aura as though you were washing a windshield and then shake them vigorously in the air. Next, imagine yourself bathed in a loving white light pouring in at the top of your head and settling into your heart. Imagine this light as an egg-shaped field about six inches away from your skin, completely enclosing your body.

While doing this, imagine everyone and every-thing that bothers you draining into the ground and away from your aura. With your eyes closed, see whose face, if any, pops into your mind. If the face of someone who has upset you shows up, then imagine that person's energy draining away from you and returning into the ground. Now imagine a golden white energy light taking its place, filling your heart and aura with peaceful feelings and a warm glow around your body.

Finally, visualize drawing energy up from the earth through the soles of your feet. Inhale deeply and visualize filling up your body with this earthy energy beginning at the bottom of your feet and going to the top of your head and then extending outward beyond your body in all directions for about five feet. Then exhale. That's it. Now you're all clear.

Aura cleaning is a favorite after-school ritual in our house. It's a cleansing that kids often need, since their world can be just as toxic and unpleasant as any adult's. This cleansing ritual gives them a way to clear away other people's vibrations and to reinforce their personal boundaries. It works when they've just failed a test or when they aren't picked for soccer. It works when their best friend won't talk to them. It works when one of them is "odd man out" and they are excluded from playgroups. It works for disappointments, letdowns, mistakes, failures, and upsets. It really does the job of clearing away negative energy and helps your children restore their auric balance. (This goes for you, too!)

INTRODUCING YOUR CHILD TO HIS AURA

You can help your children become more conscious of negativity or unpleasant energy if you teach them to actually *feel* their auras. It's easy enough to do.

Start by asking your child to place his feet solidly on the ground and find his center of balance. Once this is done, have him shake his hands out freely and then breathe in very deeply. Upon exhaling, have

him face his hands palm to palm about half an inch
apart in front of his chest and slowly move them in
circles, close but not touching each other. Ask him if
he can feel any energy moving between his palms.

Do this exercise with your child. You'll be delighted with this experience. Both you and your child should be able to feel the vibrating flow
of energy passing gently between your palms. This flow of energy may
feel warm or it may feel cool. It will feel like "thicker air."

Close your eyes and continue to pull your palms
apart until you no longer feel the vibration between
them. How far apart is this? Some kids will be able
to pull their palms up to eighteen to twenty inches
apart before the vibration begins to fade. Now
stand facing your child and face your palms toward
each other and feel the energy passing between you.
The energy you feel *is* your aura.

If your children can't feel their aura while doing this palm-to-palm
exercise, another way to help them feel it is by giving them a backrub
very slowly, with their eyes closed, and then very gently lifting your
hands off their skin an inch or two and just stroking their aura. Doing
this a few times usually awakens sensitivity. Afterward, try the hand
exercise again. If a child just can't feel her aura, then forget it—it
doesn't really matter. Just knowing about it will heighten your children's
awareness whether they can feel it or not.

OUR AURA IS LIKE A SPONGE

Explain to your children that this energy field is like a sponge and can
easily absorb the energy of others and energy in the atmosphere. If they
are around positive energy, they may absorb it, and the same with negative energy. That's why it's very important to keep from absorbing
energy you don't want to feel.

Another way to cleanse negative energy is with a technique called grounding. Grounding means literally connecting your awareness to the ground. Running, jumping, exercising, touching the dirt, hugging trees, smelling flowers—all these activities will ground the energy in the body and pull out unwanted negativity.

It's also important to "squeeze out" any negative energy that has been picked up and replace it with clear, positive energy. Children can do this by rubbing their hands together, then running them through their energy field as if raking out the debris, and finally shaking off their hands. This is a favorite technique for many massage therapists because it does the job well. You can do this to your kids, and kids can do this to each other and to you.

Usually children accept the notion of auras very easily because they do feel them, although they often don't know what to call this feeling. Knowing how to feel and clear their aura will help protect them from bullies as well. For example, Sonia is very eager to grow up and likes to play with older kids who might take advantage of her. One day I said to her, "Honey, I know you like to play with these older kids, which is fine with me, but if you do play with them, you need to know how to keep yourself from being pushed around."

"How can I, Mom? What should I do?"

"Well, anytime you begin to feel uncomfortable with a friend, you can always excuse yourself and tell him or her that you need some fresh air. Then go outside and rub your hands together and shake off the energy, and pull in fresh energy from the earth."

"What if it's cold or snowing? Or I'm on a sleepover?"

"Then go to the bathroom and shut the door. Shake out the energy, take in a deep breath, and then wash your hands and face. If you ever get to the point where this doesn't help, then just come home."

ESTABLISHING BOUNDARIES

One of the most important things a child learns in life is to set boundaries so that others will not manipulate him. Teaching children to feel their auras, to be aware of how other people's energy affects them, to clean away the energy that they don't like, or to walk away from it at any time if they must will give them tools of intuitive self-care. Some parents ask, "Why don't you just prevent your children from being exposed to negative people and circumstances?" Well, up to a point you can and should, but realistically, you can't possibly field every single negative person or situation your children may encounter before it affects them. Doing so shields them from life itself. To attempt this is to become a control freak, which will only make your children resent you. It's much better to teach children intuitive self-defense and give them tools they can use anywhere, anytime, on their own, to identify trouble and move away from its source.

PERSONAL EMPOWERMENT

A client, Grace, told me how ever since she introduced her son, Everett, to auras and personal energy fields and showed him how to establish boundaries, he has become more conscious of how other people affect him. Now, at age eleven, he can discern for himself if someone's energy bothers him, and he will freely move away from that person by himself if he doesn't like how their energy feels to him. He has gradually moved away from kids who dominated him and has found more comfortable and balanced playmates and friends. This has been his own conscious choice arising from the awareness of how different people influence him.

This summer, for example, Everett had his first sleepover camp experience. During the week he was at camp, he felt bothered by one of the boys whenever he came near. He didn't like his energy. It felt angry, aggressive, even dangerous and unsettled. Before they even spoke he'd move away.

On the second to last day of camp, after Everett had once again maneuvered away, the boy picked up a large rock and threw it at another unsuspecting child, striking her full force in the back. Then he started laughing, even though he had really hurt her. He was reprimanded and put on serious probation, which included not being allowed to go anywhere near the other kids for the rest of the day. His display of aggression was serious, and apparently it wasn't the first time, according to the counselor, who apologized for him. He had hurt another child in another incident the year before and was allowed back into camp only after much persuasion on the part of his parents. Who knows why that boy was so angry and aggressive; that wasn't for Everett to figure out. Nonetheless, Everett had been right to avoid him. Had his mom been clearing his path for him all along, I wonder whether he would have been able to choose to step away from danger on his own with as much awareness and determination. His mother was so happy to learn that he had such a keen sense of his own boundaries. It helped her to rest easier as a parent.

TAKE TOXIC ENERGY OUTSIDE

I've also taught my children to be aware of how their energy affects others—namely me! I've explained to them that fighting and squabbling, instead of trying to communicate, create toxic energy that I can't bear, and if they must do it, they have to take it outside and clear their auras before coming back in. Though this makes them mad, it also makes them conscious. They rarely want to take their differences outside, especially in cold weather, so they are more willing to negotiate their quarrels in a civilized fashion. Of course, the same rules apply to Patrick and me. If we argue (and like all married people, we do), we try to remember to be considerate enough to keep our negativity away from them, and if we forget, they have the right to remind us. Arguments and disagreements are bound to happen in any home. This in itself is less a problem than all the emotion being discharged into a closed space during an argument. The negativity bounces around the room and will settle into the atmosphere, preventing people from reaching accord or starting the argument all over again.

One way to clear the air between you and a family member is to actually take your disagreements into the clear air outdoors. Not only will the earth have a grounding and calming effect, but the energy will be dispersed into the atmosphere and not left hanging in the closets and corners.

The best tool of protection you can ever offer your kids is consciousness. Teaching them how to be conscious of their energy, to be self-loving, to be selective in what they allow to affect them, and to be proficient at clearing their energy will give them tools to keep them safe in the world.

One final word: Being conscious of energy and clearing auras is an excellent housekeeping tool for intuitive self-care, but if your child is really down or depressed, or isn't engaging with the world in a positive way, an aura cleaning will *not* take the place of counseling or therapy or medication if it is needed. Have enough awareness of your children to sense the difference between a simple case of psychic pollution and a full-blown case of physical, emotional, or mental problems.

Use your intuition and common sense when it comes to your children's psychic well-being. Giving them tools of self-care is essential for balance, but know when they need tools and when they need a skilled caretaker.

Tool THE AURA CLEANSING STOMP

It is said that when you dance your spirit fully descends into your body, bringing healing to every fiber and cell.

To cleanse your aura and energize your spirit, pick your favorite foot-stomping music. This can be rock 'n' roll, rockabilly, Zydeco, reggae, disco, Motown—any music that is energetic, *happy*, and motivating. Turn the music up as loud as the stereo (and you) can handle and dance barefoot until you're ready to drop. This is a *very* soul-cleansing family activity that will clear away negativity and refresh your spirits!

Try to dance a few times throughout the week, and pay attention to how it feels.

Tool WALK IT OFF

Nothing clears an aura and calms negativity more effectively than a walk in nature. This is so effective for aura balancing that you and your children may want to incorporate a short walk into your daily routine. Even twice around the block will be sufficient to drain away interference, eliminate psychic pollution, and restore clarity in your auric field.

Tool SHAKE YOUR WOOLIES OUT

As you know, the "woolies" are sticky, icky feelings that leave you feeling irritated. Children can get woolies from kids they don't like, from riding the bus, or even from walking by an uncomfortable place. In fact, children can pick up woolies from any unpleasant atmosphere or situation, leaving them feeling anxious, irritable, restless, and uncomfortable. If your child has the woolies, try this exercise:

> Ask your child to jump up and down (preferably outside!) for one or two minutes. (Jump ropes are great for this.) Next, ask her to close her eyes and place both feet firmly together on the ground.
> Next, ask her to breathe in and out very deeply and slowly and pretend that she is a tree. Tell her to imagine the energy from the earth climbing up through her roots, her trunk, her branches, her leaves, and on out into space.

During this exercise, guide your child through this imagery one step at a time, all the while asking her to breathe slowly in and out, until she feels clear of all "wooly" energy.

Tool HEALING HURT FEELINGS

One of the hardest things for parents is to see their children experience pain, disappointment, rejection, loss, or even cruelty. These upsets can come from mean playmates, insensitive teachers, and even irresponsible parents. Pride or fear often prevents children from openly displaying their hurt feelings when they do experience such difficulties, but this doesn't mean that they don't hurt or that they are all right.

If you notice your children suffering from psychic wounds or emotional pain, try this exercise to help them recover their balance and inner joy:

Ask your child to be quiet, close his eyes, and breathe deeply and slowly. Then ask:

Where is your sadness? (Have him point to or touch the spot in his body that is holding the sadness.)

What color is your sadness? (Ask him to give it a color.)

What shape is your sadness? (Ask him to describe its shape.)

How heavy is your sadness? (Let him compare it to something else he can pick up or measure by weight.)

Turn to your heart and ask your sadness what it wants. (Let him tune inward and listen to what he needs.)

Now, together, let's send love and healing feelings to your sadness so you can feel happy again.

Now rub your hands together and gently place them on your child's sad spot. Close your eyes and use your creative visualization to send your child a loving, healing white light pouring through your hands into his wounded place. Ask the love of the Universe to move through you to help heal your child's heavy heart.

Do this for one or two minutes, depending on how restless your child is, asking him to breathe in and out easily all the while, receiving your love.

After two minutes or so, gently remove your hands and give your child a big hug and kiss, telling him that you love him.

$\mathcal{Tool}$ WASH IT AWAY

Cleanse a troubled energy away by taking an Epsom salt bath, a technique I learned from my sister Cuky, who is a massage therapist and trance healer.

To do this, fill a tub up to the top with hot water and add three cups of Epsom salts. Have your child soak in this bath until the water is cool, then rinse her off in the shower.

This is a fantastic way to clear away a toxic or negative vibration as well as toxins in the body, and thanks to its relaxing effect, it will bring on a wonderful night's sleep.

$\mathcal{Tool}$ AROMATHERAPY

Aromatherapy is another very effective way to keep a child's aura clear. Lavender, bergamot, and chamomile are especially effective. A drop on a pillow or a few drops in a bath can clear the vibration, calm and soothe an agitated soul, and clear away toxic vibes.

$\mathcal{Tool}$ WHAT COLOR ARE YOU?

Yet another revealing way to check a child's energy field is to have him lie down on a big piece of paper, like white butcher paper, and outline his body. Then give him a big box of crayons and have him color in his own energy field. If he chooses bright, clear colors, then his energy field is fine. If he colors in black, brown, or muddy colors, have him take an Epsom salt bath and put a little lavender on his pillow or in an aromatherapy diffuser placed in his room. It will help to clear away psychic debris.

Tool BACK OFF, LITTLE BUDDY

If you are in need of space and your children won't give it to you, gently but firmly explain to them that you need a few moments of quiet to regain your energy. And then *take* it.

Ask your children to play quietly or read a book or even watch TV for the next few minutes while you reenergize. Your children may balk at this suggestion, or even test you, but if you feel truly determined to take a few moments for yourself without guilt, they will feel it intuitively and respect you, even if they are babies.

> Sit down in a chair, close your eyes, put your feet
> flat on the floor, and take in a quiet, deep breath.
> As you exhale, concentrate on quieting your mind
> and breathing evenly. Do this for a full five minutes.
> Do not rush through this centering exercise. A few
> moments of peace will keep you patient and in
> harmony with your children. Everyone will be
> better off.

Reflections

1. Have you felt your own aura? Describe it.

_____

_____

_____

2. Are you becoming more conscious of your children's auras? How?

_____

_____

_____

3. Have you introduced your child to his aura? What happened?

_____

_____

_____

4. Have you tried any aura cleansing techniques? Which ones?

_____

_____

_____

5. Which works best for you?

_____

_____

_____

6. Which works best for your children?

_____

_____

_____

7. Are you able to identify a toxic aura? Your own? Your child's? Others? Give an example.

_____

_____

_____

8. Are you willing to take steps to clear it? What tools have you used in doing so?

_____

_____

_____

9. Have you asked your children whether they can see your aura? Or their own?

_____

_____

_____

10. If they have, ask them what color it was.

_____

_____

_____

11. If they haven't, ask them what color they feel it is.

_____

_____

_____

12. Ask yourself the same thing.

_____

_____

_____

13. Do your children feel any differently having learned how to clear an aura of negative energy? Describe.

_____

_____

_____

Talk about auras with your children and ask them to "check in" with their aura often.

REMINDERS

Are you:

    Keeping your house clutter free and serene?

    Noticing the subtle and tuning in to vibration?

    Creating your own language of spirit?

    Remembering to clear your aura and those of your children?

EIGHT

Blind Spots and Bad Habits

I constantly remind parents that creating an awareness of intuition is only part of the equation for living an intuitive life. The other part is having the willingness and flexibility to accept and respond to intuition fully when it does show up. Unless you can fully embrace the subtle guiding messages you and your children receive and act accordingly, its value and benefits will not be felt. Intuition is a gift, but it is up to you to accept the gift. This means that you may at times have to change plans, give up old habits, break with tradition, rock the boat, challenge authority, or reverse your direction and beliefs in life.

The function of intuition is to make better decisions and to prevent us from making costly or disruptive mistakes. Intuition serves to direct our attention to the best ways of achieving goals, alerts us to potential problems and dangers, and acts to protect us and keep us safely on our path. Therefore it makes perfect sense that an intuitive feeling—especially a child's intuitive feeling—may likely call for a change of direction or ask you to rethink your ideas on things.

This is a very important message for parents because one of the greatest blocks to a child's intuitive awakening usually lies in a parent's unconscious or automatic inclination to tune out their children's insights as a matter of habit. Even parents who are committed to encouraging the development of their children's intuition can fall prey to negative tendencies. As human beings, we are all creatures of habit. Especially when it comes to intuition, some of our inherited habits contain blind spots that interfere with our goals.

INTUITION IS REAL

My friend Julia recounted this story to me one day.

Her daughter Domenica had just arrived home after a year away at college. Shortly after unpacking her bags, she mentioned to her mother that she had "a creepy feeling" that someone was watching her. Julia dismissed it, thinking that Domenica was simply feeling unsettled after being away at school. After all, they lived well outside their small New Mexico town in a safe and very sparsely populated area.

The next night Domenica came into her mother's bedroom, again saying that she had the terrible feeling someone was watching her. She asked whether Julia would mind if she slept in the room with her that night. Julia saw that Domenica was really upset and moved over in the bed, but she never once considered that someone might indeed be watching.

The third night Domenica, now chastising herself for being paranoid, went back to her room and undressed for bed. In the reflection of her mirror she saw a hooded man crouched outside the window, watching her. She screamed loudly enough to wake the dead, and her mother came running. The Peeping Tom ran off, and Julia called the police.

Someone *had* been watching Domenica for the past three days, and she wasn't the only one. Several other people had reported him to the police during the same period. What alarmed Julia about the situation was that even though she was sensitive to her daughter's insecurities and was more than willing to comfort her, she had never once considered that Domenica's feelings might be valid.

"I wasn't *intending* to disbelieve her or discount her feelings," Julia said. "It just came automatically."

In another instance my friend Carol told me a story that concerned her son Nile. She said that many years ago, when Nile was eight or nine years old and they were living in the country, their family dog, Bowser, disappeared. Carol and Nile were terribly upset; they searched for him everywhere, to no avail.

Five nights after Bowser's disappearance Carol attended an important dinner party. Nile called Carol at the party and said, "Mom, I hear some breathing outside. I think it's Bowser. Can you please come home?"

"Nile, I honestly don't see how you could hear Bowser breathing from indoors," Carol said. "You know we've looked everywhere around the house. I think it's just your imagination. Please go back to bed."

A few days later a hired hand from the farm next door appeared to tell them that he had found Bowser lying next to the pipes where pesticides were pumped into the irrigation system. The poison lay puddled there, and Bowser had been drinking it. The saddest part was that had Carol acted on Nile's call, perhaps Bowser could have been saved.

Neither Julia nor Carol was consciously discounting their children's intuition. It happened automatically. Their reactions were just part of an ingrained culture that invalidates children's intuitive feelings (or anyone's, for that matter) without thought. As good mothers their concern was more about making the "bad" feeling go away and not changing the program than about asking themselves what the feeling was about. They preferred to focus on reassuring their children that all was well, rather than considering that their children were messengers of important information.

LISTEN AND BELIEVE

Kids experience spontaneous intuitive messages more readily than adults do, and as parents we need to listen to them. After years of indoctrination to look for what the agenda calls for—for what *seems* to be instead of what *is*—our own intuitive edge begins to dull. In kids, this instinct to discern what's what is usually pretty keen. A good way to keep your children's instincts sharp, as well as to reactivate your own, is to respect their first impressions, listen to their vibes, allow their natural responses, and encourage them to share these feelings with you. Treat their feelings as valid, and believe what they are telling you even if it seems unlikely or puts you in an uncomfortable or even awkward position.

A simple change in our awareness and habits of what to do when our children express intuitive feelings can create tremendous break-throughs in awakening and validating this gift in them as well as reacti-vating your own. Take all intuitive feelings seriously, and pay attention to what your children are saying and what they want to do, or to what you want to do. Kids get vibes from somewhere, and if you recognize these vibes as an important response to energy, then you'll understand how a sensitive mind picks up such energy. In fact, a child's clear mind often picks up on things adults overlook or filter out because they don't want to know. Children do tune in to what we tune out, and they need you to reflect back to them that what they tune in to matters.

BE RESPECTFUL

Last winter, out of the blue, Sabrina started complaining about being scared to sleep in her own bed and begged me to let her sleep in our room. After a few nights of this, I told her I would prefer that she sleep in her room and that we needed to get to the bottom of her fears.

Tearfully she got into her own bed and said, "I'm sorry, Mom. I don't know what the problem is! It's just that I have bad vibes."

I sat on the bed and tried to help her sort out these feelings. I have had hundreds of bad vibe attacks myself, and they do make me want to jump out of my skin, especially when the uneasy feeling is so vague that I don't have any idea what's causing it.

I decided to do an exercise with her that my mom used to do with me when I had bad feelings as a child. I focused my attention on her vibes and said, "Sabrina, close your eyes, listen to your heart, and ask yourself what your worry is about. Can you tell who or what your feel-ing is about?"

"I don't know!" she cried with her eyes closed. "I'm just worried that something could happen to one of us. Like Sonia or you."

"Well, Sabrina, if that's what your vibes tell you, then we'd better say prayers and visualize white light surrounding all of us for protection," I answered.

Sabrina thought this was a great suggestion, and together we did just that. Then I massaged her feet for a few minutes to calm her down and sat in her room until she went to sleep. By the time I got to bed it was late. This was the fourth night in a row of bad vibes, and I had to admit I wondered whether she was creating drama just to be the center of attention, which she was capable of doing, or if she really was getting a warning. Yet experience has taught me that it is always better to listen and respect a vibe, no matter whose it is. For added measure I made a note to myself to keep a protective shield around all of us for the next couple of days.

When we woke up the next morning the ground was covered in a beautiful, fresh blanket of snow. On the spur of the moment Patrick and I decided to take the girls skiing at a ski area an hour away from our house. In the car Sabrina mentioned her vibes one more time, and we all agreed that meant we needed to be extra careful that day.

Once there we had a splendid time. Patrick had taught each of the girls how to ski when they were only three years old, so they are very comfortable on the hill. After a while, as Sonia and I approached the chair lift, we noticed the lift seemed to be going faster than it should. Before we were ready the chairs flew up behind our legs and scooped us up. Sonia's skis got tangled, and she suddenly flipped off and fell a few feet to the ground. She popped her head up as soon as she landed.

"Get down!" I screamed at her, dangling from the chair, and instantly she dived back down, just in time for the oncoming chair to miss her head.

The chair lift operator slammed off the machine and dragged Sonia over to the side as I jumped off the lift and stumbled over to her. A bit bruised, we limped off to the lodge, shaken but relieved that we had avoided a terrible accident.

Once inside, hot chocolate in hand, Sonia said to me, "Do you think this is what Sabrina was picking up on the last few nights?"

I nodded. Even though her warnings did not prevent an accident from happening, I'm certain that having been alerted and on our toes that day because of them kept us from having a serious accident. We decided that since Sonia was all right, we wouldn't ruin the fun for Patrick and Sabrina by telling them about the accident until later. When we told them on the way home Sabrina's eyes popped open. "So that's what I was feeling!"

We'll never know for sure. All I know is that Sabrina slept soundly that night without any fuss at all.

BAD VIBES AND BAD NEWS BEARS

Sometimes kids' bad vibes center around the people we are the least suspicious of. They may even be friends or family members. As adults we may have a hard time believing that someone we know and like is not really safe to be around.

One of my clients named Ron recounted a frustrating experience he had as a teenager when Jim, the husband of his mom's best friend, Irene, gave him bad vibes. Jim had been married to Irene a long time and was considered a good friend of the family. When Ron was eleven years old Jim started visiting the family while on an annual business trip. To all appearances Jim was an easygoing, nice guy, but Ron could never really let his guard down around him. He kept his distance from Jim, although he couldn't put his finger on exactly what the problem was. Ron's younger brothers, nine-year-old Sam and ten-year-old Howie, loved Jim and didn't share Ron's suspicion in spite of Ron's warnings to "watch out" every time he came to the house.

One summer when Jim was visiting, he started wrestling with Howie in the yard, but after a few minutes he pinned him to the ground and wouldn't let him move. Ron, watching from the back porch, got really upset. He ran out of the house and pulled Jim off Howie ferociously, screaming, "Get off him *right now*!"

Jim, Howie, and Ron's mother and father, who heard Ron yelling, looked at him as if he had gone crazy. He was seriously lectured for being so rude and sent to his room.

"I'll never forget the moment when I pulled Jim off," Ron said. "Jim's and my eyes locked for an instant, then *he* looked away. That visit was the last for Jim. After that he lost touch with us."

One day some years later Ron came home from school and was met by his mom, who had an odd look on her face.

"I got a surprising telephone call from Irene today," she said. "She told me that her husband, Jim, was arrested. Apparently he was accused of molesting a neighborhood kid. We are *so* shocked!"

Ron threw his books on the floor. "Son of a gun! I *tried* to tell you he was weird, but you guys wouldn't listen to me!"

"It's true," Ron's mother said, "you sensed something we didn't." Ron told me that his parents apologized that day, grateful that Jim hadn't hurt Ron or his two brothers.

Believe it or not, Ron's experience is not uncommon. I've talked to hundreds of people who say that when they were kids they had bad vibes about someone, and instead of being listened to, they were completely ignored or quickly dismissed and sometimes even punished for suggesting that anything was out of order. When kids have intimations of danger or dishonesty, parents' reactions can easily slip into one of several responses. One is to "shoot the messenger," as Ron's parents did. Another response is to try to change your child's feeling. This happens when your child has a negative feeling about someone and you don't want to hear about it because you like the person in question.

RAINING ON THE PARADE

My friend Renee gave me another example of this. A single mother raising her only child, Laura, age six, Renee didn't have much of a love life, so she was delighted when she met a man she really clicked with. Renee thought Fred was a perfect gentleman, yet Laura didn't like him.

At first Renee suspected Laura felt competitive with Fred and that time would change her mind, but it didn't. Renee told Laura how kind Fred was and how much she enjoyed his company, but that didn't work, either. Laura still didn't like Fred. Finally, an exasperated Renee decided that Laura was just being stubborn and chose to ignore her, because she liked Fred, and at the time that was all that mattered to her. She continued to see him and was very excited about a possible future with him.

Renee was in love.

After another month passed Renee received a call at work from Fred's wife! She couldn't believe he had a *wife*. When she confronted Fred he finally admitted it was true, he was married.

"All I could think of was how Laura had been right all along. Fred wasn't as he appeared, and she felt it. I told Laura I was sorry that I so readily discounted her. I believed what I wanted to believe. Laura believed what was true.

"Later, when I met Herb, Laura liked him right away. She didn't mind when he came over, laughed at his jokes, and even teased us when we went out on dates. We've been married for three years now, and I feel we're a real family."

As was the case with Ron's parents and with Renee, it can be very easy to shut down or deny our own or someone else's sensory awareness when we want to believe the best about a person. Perhaps because they are so little and depend so heavily on adults for protection, kids' sensory awareness is usually set on "high" when it comes to their instincts.

I think we should never ignore any vibe a child has. My friend Phyllis once said to me, "It's hard to tell when they're young what to listen to. So much of what they say is just imagination."

"True," I said, "but all intuition arises out of the imagination. Better to pay attention to all of it than to ignore and to regret it later."

Recognizing a child's bad vibes is one way to keep her and often yourself out of harm's way. Kids who are well grounded and confident that they will be listened to respectfully when expressing themselves are usually avoided by the creepsters and opportunists of life. My teachers taught me, "Being listened to and respected is a natural form of protection in life."

BETTER SAFE THAN SORRY

My friend Amy told me about an intuitive experience she had as a child that caused a lot of upset. When Amy was three years old, visiting her grandparents in Michigan with the family, her parents bought an Oldsmobile secondhand from them, planning to drive it back home to Long Island.

As soon as the family was loaded into the car and on the road, Amy began to act out. Because she was never one to throw a tantrum, this behavior was very unlike her. She kicked and screamed, saying she hated the car, and refused to settle down. This went on for some time and began to upset her parents, especially since her other four siblings were dozing off. Finally, Amy's mother insisted that her father pull into a service station so they could try to calm Amy down. Amy's mother ran Amy to the bathroom and tried to settle her a bit, to no avail. Amy screamed that she hated the car and threw herself down on the ground and refused to get up.

Amy's father, out of patience, tried to pull her up, but Amy's mother suddenly stopped him. She knew this behavior was absolutely out of character for Amy, and her own intuition told her that perhaps there was something wrong. She asked her husband to have the car checked out to see if anything might be malfunctioning.

Amy's father agreed. Anything to stop this scene and get going.

Much to their shock, the service man found a silver dollar–size hole in the fuel line, which was causing carbon monoxide to leak back into the car. That explained why Amy's three sisters and brother had dozed off so quickly.

"If you'd carried on for another few hours, you might all have been dead," the attendant said in a most dramatic fashion. "Thank God you noticed! What a miracle."

All eyes were on Amy, only this time with complete amazement and appreciation.

Is it a hassle to pay attention to kids' intuition? It can be—but not nearly as much as the consequences of ignoring them! This doesn't mean that we should become hypervigilant around what children say. That too would be unnatural and place uncomfortable attention on our children. Simply listen to them if they do express uneasiness about anything, and if they have bad vibes, let them know that you are aware, you'll pay attention, what they feel is important, and you will do what you can to change the situation if necessary.

GETTING TOO FAMILIAR

There is a difference between bad vibes and simply protecting oneself with a natural reserve. We all start out in life with six senses, including our intuition. One of the functions of intuition is to keep us safe and out of harm's way. It scans our environment and alerts us to anything that is different from or other than our own energy field. In children, these differences elicit a natural reserve. When they encounter a new person or situation, they must first familiarize themselves with the new energy before they open up. This is why babies, for example, turn their eyes away when a stranger looks too closely at them. If they feel the energy coming toward them from the new person is friendly, they may gradually steal a peek. Otherwise they may simply avoid eye contact. As they adjust to the energy and become more comfortable, they will open up to the new person or situation naturally, in their own time, at their own pace.

I have a very outgoing friend named Alan who has a two-year-old daughter named Jennifer. Alan greets everyone with a smile, while Jennifer runs behind his legs and peeks out. Alan is constantly encouraging Jennifer to come out and say hello, especially in elevators. I suggested to Alan that he stop doing that, since it isn't instinctively natural for two-year-olds to address strangers. By suggesting that Jennifer do so, Alan was scrambling her natural instinctive boundaries and causing her unnecessary anxiety.

When parents interfere with this process, pushing children quickly into communication with unfamiliar people, they override children's natural instincts, and children lose touch with them. When this happens they become vulnerable. No wonder kids grow into adults who ignore their instincts and simply go along with appearances. No wonder this leads to trouble in adult life. If we lose touch with our instincts, we can end up associating with people who do not have our best interests at heart—and not know it until it's too late, as in the case of the business partner who takes advantage of us or the friend who betrays us.

Another mixed message we give our children often comes in our expectations of what is polite behavior. When we take our children to visit friends or relatives we often say, "Give Aunt Mary a kiss," or,

"Give Uncle Joe a hug," only to have our children recoil or resist, embarrassing us and making the children feel rude.

The truth is that spontaneous affection with strangers, even those we are related to, is also very unnatural, and the intuitive instinct to refrain from such forced intimacy is quite correct. We need to assess a person's energy and discern whether or not we are comfortable with it before we open ourselves up to it. This is true for ourselves and even more so for children. After all, *as* children they are more vulnerable than adults, so they need to be intuitively more cautious. Therefore, respect your children's natural boundaries and offer more comfortable and self-respecting ways to be polite. A simple "Say hello to so-and-so" is just as polite and much more appropriate than forcing an unwanted hug.

It takes attention and sensitivity to remember that children are much more honest and comfortable with creating an energetic balance than we give them credit for. All it takes is a little creativity and a little common sense of our own to make whatever adjustments are necessary in any given situation. It is much easier to do this if we remember that our intuitive requirements, and those of our kids, are just as real and as important as our need for food, water, and oxygen and require the same as those physical needs.

LET THEM SPEAK FOR THEMSELVES

I know a woman who has several children and loves them greatly, but every time we visit them a curious thing happens. I might say to the oldest, who is eleven, "How are you, Lucy?" But before Lucy can even open her mouth, her mother chimes in with, "Oh, she's just fine, thank you. Aren't you, Lucy?" Then Lucy will smile and stand there passively. Or I might say, "How is school this year?" and up pipes Mom with, "Terrific, she's having a great time, isn't that right, Lucy?" And Lucy just nods, with her eyes on Mom.

I know that Lucy's mother is attempting to teach her the art of conversation, but in answering for Lucy, she is really communicating to her daughter a vote of no confidence in Lucy's ability to respond and express her own feelings. Or perhaps she doesn't want Lucy to express dissatisfied feelings. Perhaps her mom's need to present a pleasant and perfect picture to the world has shut down Lucy's own ability to feel and express *real* feelings. Perhaps it's a habit she learned as a child herself, who knows?

All I do know is that when it comes to Lucy's feelings, rather than checking with herself, Lucy checks with her mother. It's as if she's saying, "Mom, tell me how I feel about that question." This can lead to real problems for Lucy in the future. At eleven she already has abandoned her own feedback system and is disconnected from her intuition.

Be patient with your children when it comes to expressing their feelings. Allow them the room to get in touch with themselves when you engage them in a conversation. Realize that usually when a child is asked, "How are you?" they believe the question is asked sincerely; therefore they are inclined to take a moment to reflect before answering. It is often in this pause that an enthusiastic parent, feeling uncomfortable with the pause, chimes in with an answer.

Exercising a little patience when talking to kids, and especially adolescents, usually reaps great rewards, both for you and for them. It allows you to connect with your children in more than a superficial way and lets them know that their feelings are important enough for you to be patient.

BAD VIBES VERSUS FEAR OF THE UNKNOWN

Just as there is a difference between bad vibes and natural reservations, so is there a distinction between bad vibes and a natural fear of the unknown. Fear of the unknown is our natural checks and balances system. It slows us down and heightens our awareness when we are exposed to potential danger. It is our most basic instinct for survival.

My friend Detective Bittenbinder calls our fear of the unknown the "hairs standing up on the back of your neck syndrome" and says it is what keeps us alive as a species. A good example of this is when you wander all alone down an unfamiliar darkened street at night. Even though this may not necessarily be harmful, it *could* be. Therefore it's likely that you will have a healthy dose of "fear of the unknown" coursing through your veins at that time.

This particular instinct varies in intensity, depending upon the situation. The more vulnerable you are, the more intensely fearful you may be. That's why some kids, especially those who are abandoned or neglected or live in violent conditions, are extremely fearful. They are in danger, and their heightened fear, by making them hypervigilant, may save their lives.

Most of the time, however, a child's fear of the unknown is based not so much on a physical threat as on a psychic upset brought about by being placed in unfamiliar circumstances or conditions that cause emotional vulnerability: when a child has a new baby-sitter, for example, or is invited to visit a new friend for the first time, or when it's time to visit the dentist, or when changing schools. Though these are not threatening or dangerous situations, a child nevertheless finds himself in ungrounded and isolating energy, leaving him feeling nervous, vulnerable, and scared.

I've seen parents become very annoyed and impatient with their children when they become afraid in obviously nonthreatening situations. A father once said to me, "My daughter is just overreacting. She needs to get over it and discover new things."

"Yes, she does," I agreed. "Yet the truth is that even though children need to experience new situations, it doesn't change the fact that energetically it *can* feel overwhelming and scary for them."

If your child has a fear of new situations, instead of saying there's nothing to be afraid of, try offering her a few understanding words to acknowledge these fears. After all, even adults can become afraid when entering uncharted waters, so why be surprised when children do?

You can calm a child's fear of the unknown in several ways. First ask your child to identify, to the best of his ability, what his fear is. Sometimes simply encouraging a child to describe what he fears reduces his anxiety and helps him put it into perspective. Another way is to suggest to your child that she visualize herself surrounded in a loving white light, protected by God and his angels. Knowing that they are in such a cocoon of protection greatly helps insecure children become more grounded and at ease and reminds them that as spiritual beings they are never truly alone, that the Universe is watching over them lovingly at all times.

You may also want to try some of the aura clearing and energy grounding techniques discussed earlier, such as the aura cleansing stomp or picking up the pieces. These tools and rituals are great for the "I want to go, I don't want to go!" ambivalent moments in life when a child's desires collide with his fears.

The best way to handle children's fear of the unknown is to be patient, matter-of-fact, and respectful and listen to what they are feeling and fearing. Don't overreact or attempt to deny what they are feeling in an effort to make them feel better. Be especially aware not to call their fears "nothing." It might be nothing physical, but it is *something* energetic and very *real* to them. Calmly ask your child what her vibes feel like and if there is anything she wants you as a parent to do. Once the child expresses her feelings, ask if she can be more specific, such as, "I know you don't care for our baby-sitter. Is there anything in particular you don't like?" Or, "I know you are afraid to go to Susie's house today. Is there anything you are specifically worried about?"

This type of focused questioning will help your child separate vague anxieties from real danger, and it reminds her that you are supportive and sensitive to her psychic state and are willing to protect her and keep her safe in the world.

FEAR OF THE DARK

Another common childhood fear is fear of the dark. Many children become terrified of the dark and can't go to sleep in a darkened room alone, convinced the "bogeyman" or some other night creature is waiting in the shadows to get them. I had a client whose son was terrified of the dark. He was a perfectly adventurous child during the day, extremely outgoing and interested in discovering new things, but come nighttime he would fall apart, begging not to be left alone. His parents didn't understand these opposing tendencies. "What is he so afraid of at night, when he's so confident during the day?" they asked.

"It could be one of several things," I said. "He might be losing touch with your personal vibration in the night, which could cause him alarm. Or he could become ungrounded in the dark and feel too wide open and vulnerable. But probably the biggest reason he has fear of the dark is that he has learned, perhaps from you, that to be safe in life, he has to be in control, and in the dark, he doesn't know what is out there, so he can't control it. This would definitely make him very afraid."

It doesn't really matter why a child has a fear of the dark. The important point is to take his fear seriously and help him overcome it and feel more secure and grounded. One solution is to let him sleep in your room. Some parents do this, believing in the "family bed." This sleeping arrangement is very common in Europe and Asia but is not too popular here in our country, where parents usually want their privacy. Another solution is to allow him to keep the lights on and the door open when he goes to bed, in order to see what's "out there," perhaps offering a night-light that isn't too bright so it doesn't disturb his ability to unwind. Another solution is to clear the energy in the room with essential oils. Chamomile is a wonderful essential oil for inducing calm and creating a relaxing atmosphere that is perfect for sleep. Another solution is to "smudge" his room with a "smudge stick." This is a wand of dried sage and cedar, available in most metaphysical bookstores. Smudge sticks are Native American energy tools, designed to clear energy and create sacred space. Smudging expels all negative vibrations, leaving the atmosphere purified and blessed. Smudging is especially effective for fearful children if you explain to them what it is, what it is used for, and even let them be the one to wave it around the room.

But the best way to reassure a child who has a fear of the dark is to let him know that the loving Universe is aware of him, is protecting him, and will watch over him during the night, just as it does during the day. Therefore he can *trust* that all is well, and he doesn't have to try to control anything. You must teach him not to worry, that the Universe is on the job and will handle things for him. The only way for you to do this, however, is to believe it yourself!

EASY DOES IT

Even though many parents err on the side of underplaying intuition's role in their children's lives, many other parents become overzealous and make too much of a fuss over it. That's very annoying to children and will shut off their intuition just as readily as ignoring it will.

One of my clients, Holly, showed up at my door one day with a three-page list of observations on her three-year-old son Timmy's intuitive abilities. She was sure every little word out of his mouth was evidence of great intuitive insight. She coached, coaxed, prodded, and hovered over him, interpreting his every response as an intuitive revelation or a deep and meaningful intuitive insight.

"Sonia, he stared at the baby-sitter for three whole minutes before he said hello," she reported. "It was as if he were reading her every inner secret. Every time we're around new people I ask Tim what color their aura is, what he's feeling, and he tells me. I think he's very intuitive, don't you?"

Of course I *did* think Tim was intuitive, and I thought Holly had the right idea to nurture his intuition. But hovering over Tim waiting for a sound-and-light show was definitely the wrong approach. It was unnatural and awkward and an invasion of her son's space, and any child would certainly intuitively feel and resent such pressure coming from a parent.

No child enjoys being treated as "different," either in front of people or behind closed doors. Children spend a great deal of energy trying to fit into society, not to be singled out from it. Even though it's just as important for parents to cultivate their children's intuitive perceptions as it is to help them appreciate music or art, it is neither helpful nor desirable to make them self-conscious. And if a parent approaches a child's intuition too seriously, it takes the fun out of it as well.

You will never connect with intuition through coercion, demands, testing, or obsessing. When you listen, you engage a child's essence, capture her soul, and tap into her spirit. When you obsess, coerce, contrive, manipulate, or demand intuitive performance from a child, you engage her ego, completely bypassing the soul. The ego doesn't have access to intuition—only the spirit does—so this kind of behavior will never make the connection to intuition that you want.

The effective approach to take toward your children's intuition is to gently appreciate it as a part of the chemistry that makes them who they are. Allow for your children to discuss every aspect of their intuitive life freely without coercing it with drama or overreaction or by treating it as something unusual.

Check your own attitude. At this point you should begin to understand that we are all thinking, feeling, sensing, intuitive beings and that our intuitive lives are just as much a part of our magnificent makeup as are our eyes and ears. Relax, allow room for intuitive exploration and discovery, and trust that it will flourish naturally.

EVERYTHING COUNTS

In summary, the most important thing to learn about responding to your children's vibes is not to shoot the messenger or let sentimentality cloud your own perspective. If they have warnings, heed them. If they express disturbances, honor them. If they show dislikes, respect them. If they need space, give it to them. If they are fearful, be sensitive and reassuring. And do it lovingly. Clear minds pick up clear vibes, and kids do have an uncannily keen sense of the obvious, so recognize their vibes as an attempt to stave off problems, keep their balance, and warn or protect themselves and you, and appreciate them for it.

Whatever you do, don't make them feel as though they are the cause of any vibes—good, bad, or indifferent. This is unfair, unkind, and untrue.

At some point in intuitive development it is important to wake up and smell the coffee if you aren't paying attention! Take off the rose-colored glasses if you wear them. Snap out of denial if you are in it, and change your plans when called for. Be glad that these little beings are using all their senses to keep life safe, balanced, and honest.

The good thing about recognizing and honoring your children's vibes, their natural boundaries, their heightened instinct for self-preservation, and their keen sense of the obvious is that by being this sensitive to their vibes, you can't help but become this sensitive to your own as well.

In a power-and-control culture such as ours, we've all been highly indoctrinated to go "with the program without question," but often doing so runs counter to listening to our heart and doing what is right for ourselves. Intuition is a gift from spirit, but it is still up to us to reach out and accept the gift when it is offered, even though it may at times be disruptive to our plans, challenge authority, or make us reevaluate people and perspectives that we are attached to. It takes courage to follow the intuitive heart and believe in the guiding wisdom of the soul, but its gifts are worth the effort.

Breaking out of unconsciousness and automatic habits and following the guiding winds of spirit, whether arising in you or in your child, no matter the consequences, is the turning point in living an intuitive life. The day that you decide to do this will be the day that your life, and that of your child's, will open up to the guiding light and abundant gifts of God's grace.

Tool OVERCOMING BLIND SPOTS AND BAD HABITS

If you *really* want your children to trust their intuition, *you* will have to trust it first. If you place enough value on what your children's instincts tell them, so will they. Try:

1. Listening to your children with an open mind.
2. Being aware of their signals and communications.
3. Allowing your children to speak freely.
4. Respecting their vibes and instincts.
5. Focusing on their body language and offering protection.
6. Being patient when they voice intuitive feelings, especially when they inconvenience you, upset your plans, or reflect something negative in someone close to you.
7. Having humor and flexibility when intuitions arise.
8. Always trusting a child's intuition—and yours, too, of course.
9. Not ignoring either your own or your child's vibes when they do show up.
10. Urging everyone in the family to speak up when it comes to vibes.

Reflections

1. Are you willing to respect your child's natural boundaries and first impressions?

2. Do you unconsciously impose rules of politeness that override your child's gut instincts?

3. Are you too busy to incorporate your child's intuition into your decisions?

4. Do you tune your children out when their intuition causes you to feel uncomfortable?

5. Are you in such a chronically negative emotional state—anxious, harried, angry—that you are out of tune with your own or your child's intuition?

REMINDERS

Are you:

Creating your own language of spirit?

Remembering to clear your aura and those of your kids?

Being respectful of all vibes, however inconvenient or unpleasant they may be?

Asking for Support

WE ARE NOW MOVING INTO THE FINAL PHASE of nurturing an intuitive family: asking for support.

In Part III you will concentrate on shifting your focus from merely being aware and accepting of intuition to actively seeking intuition's counsel in your life. You will do this by

1. Creating an atmosphere of wonder and discovery.

2. Introducing your children to the importance of asking for guidance.

3. Using art as a way to reach the intuitive heart.

4. Finding ways to encourage your children to focus inward and expect guidance from their soul.

5. Meeting your helpers and guides.

6. Understanding how the body is temporary but the soul is eternal.

You and your children are about to shift from a life that is ordinary, ego based, and afraid into one that is extraordinary, spiritually directed, and secure. Continue your efforts, knowing that soon you and your family will reclaim the guiding wisdom of your souls!

NINE

Creating Wonder and Discovery

I was talking last week with my friend Bill, who has just recently reclaimed his intuitive voice after a long silence. In describing his experience, he said, "It's like discovering a muscle you didn't know you had. First you have to find it, then you have to use it!"

It's true. Using intuition is like using a new muscle. At first you may resist, or it may feel odd, but with practice intuitive feelings get stronger and more comfortable to reach for. Intuition is a subtle feeling, a quick flash of "ah-hah!" It's the light bulb going on in your head. The "I just know" that all of us have had a million and one times flitting by like a feather brushing our cheeks.

But as so many upstanding members of the "woulda-coulda-shoulda" club of intuitive hindsight will testify, knowing something intuitively and having the *confidence* to act on the knowledge are two entirely different things. As my friend Bill put it, "It's hard to use your intuition sometimes. You get so anxious about making a mistake, it paralyzes you." And he's right. It can be unnerving to go by your intuition, especially when big decisions are involved. What's nerve-racking about making a mistake is that all too often we demand perfection of ourselves.

The best way to avoid blocked intuition is to learn *how* to use those intuitive muscles freely and without censure or consequence as we grow up. The anxious feeling Bill spoke of, that fear of making mistakes, actually settles in during childhood. This is the time when a child is either encouraged to explore and allowed the opportunity to goof up without dire consequences or is penalized for his mistakes and becomes too afraid to take any chances. How your child feels about taking risks, especially intuitive ones, will be largely determined by your behavior.

If you are a parent who is heavily goal oriented, evaluates your self-worth by your performance, and doesn't tolerate mistakes, chances are that your children will also strive for success the same way in order to gain your approval. Such circumstances create fear in children, making it very tough for them to access intuition. Whenever we are fearful, the fear overrides our intuition or drowns it out completely, and that is how we grow up listening to our fears instead of our hearts.

I've noticed an alarming number of ambitious baby boomer parents driven by the need for their children to be the best—not at what the *children* can be, but at what the *parents* think they should be. They push, cajole, threaten, even dictate that their children be top performers. I've seen children as young as six or seven comparing themselves with one another based on their grades, their extracurricular activities, even how well they play a musical instrument. I know a gifted piano teacher who has stopped having piano recitals because of the competition, aggression, and fear of failing her students display during recitals. "You know, it's the parents causing all this stress," she says. "Kids don't act like this naturally. Kids learn to act like this."

With so many children carrying the burden of their parents' expectations and ambitions on their small shoulders at younger and younger ages, it's no wonder that fear becomes their guiding voice. The best way to ensure that your children grow up motivated by a strong sense of inner guidance rather than fear as a motivator is to create as many opportunities as possible for them to flex their intuitive muscles. This means fostering a sense of play, adventure, discovery, and wonder. We need to allow our children to awaken their intuitive knowing through delightful opportunities, where they can experiment with what they love and express what they feel without risk of censure or failure—or, worst of all, loss of your love.

THE I WONDER GAME

Because intuition operates best through the doorway of the imagination, the best way to access it is through creative play. When I was very young we had lots of kids and little money. Our lives were lived on a lean budget, but my mother had an incredible knack for turning the ordinary into the extraordinary and everyday events into magic-making moments. One of the ways she did this was playing a game called I Wonder. "Wonder is a magic word," she used to say. "When you wonder you play with the Universe!" I Wonder was like a guessing game, only we weren't simply guessing—we actually were wondering.

When the phone rang my mother would ask, "I wonder who's on the phone? Don't you?" And we'd close our eyes and wonder. Was it Dad? Was it my mom's best friend, Charlotte? Was it Grandma? Then we closed our eyes and tried to *feel* who was calling. It was fun to send our minds on such delightful adventures. We would each take a turn naming the caller before we would pick up the phone. When we found out who it was, we'd cheer ourselves on if we had been right, and we'd laugh if we were wrong. It didn't matter—after all, it was just a game.

Another I Wonder opportunity came in the grocery store. I wonder what's on special today? I wonder where the best apples are? I wonder what Dad wants for dinner? Wondering through our days became part of our lives. We'd wonder what the school lunch was. We'd wonder when the pop quizzes were. We'd wonder what the answers were. It became a natural way of navigating through the day.

I've spent my whole life wondering. It's opened my eyes and pointed my nose in the right direction thousands of times. The best part is that it has helped me approach situations with an open mind and heart. Growing up with wonder sets the tone to approach life that way. It's a hard habit to break—it's too much fun, and it makes life work better.

It helps when you wonder who people really are instead of judging by appearances. It helps when you wonder how to best do your work instead of falling into a rut. Above all, wonder directs your attention to options that you might have otherwise overlooked, and it keeps your awareness fresh and keen.

You can play I Wonder with kids of any age. It teaches them to explore the unseen world with the same enthusiasm that they bring to their physical surroundings. It helps them access the unknown, the spiritual and intuitive side of life and of themselves. And the best part is that it's fun.

You can play I Wonder anywhere, anytime, but it works best when a kid is wondering about something she is really interested in. Sonia wonders on the piano, trying to play songs she's heard on the radio that she enjoys. Sabrina wonders how to draw things and people in ancient times. We all wonder where our keys and shoes and backpacks and coats are from time to time, and we all have a great time letting wonder guide us.

When you play I Wonder, there are several rules to follow. The first is that you can't be wrong, because it's not a test. If you let it become a test, it loses its magic. The second rule is that when you are wrong or wander off course, you say, "Oh well!" and laugh. Then wonder some more. That way there are no negative consequences to wondering. And the last rule is that when you wonder into a positive solution or outcome, you celebrate—a lot!

Encourage your kids to play I Wonder early in life. Lay out the rules clearly. When they break them (and you can count on it, because competition is everywhere), help them back off and regroup. Introduce I Wonder whenever you can and invite their ideas on new ways to wonder. This is a marvelous way to access inspiration, insight, creativity, and intuition, and it will help you as a family always to be open to new experiences.

TRAVEL AND ADVENTURE

Another way to encourage intuitive muscles is to introduce a sense of adventure into your family life through travel. Patrick and I are avid travelers, and whenever we can we take our children with us. Traveling introduces them to new situations, new customs, new food, and new people. It shows them that there are many different ways to live life and develop curiosity and an open mind. Travel heightens awareness, sharpens the instincts, turns the sensory apparatus on "high," and usually jump-starts the intuition because intuition thrives on new and unknown circumstances. Parents are now traveling with kids in record numbers, even to the point of taking them out of school to do so. To this I say, terrific!

My own intuition went from moderately activated to full-blown intuitive knowing when I had my first adventure at the age of sixteen. I have always been fascinated with my mother's history and her Romanian background. When I was six, my mother returned to Romania and was reunited with her family, sixteen years after the war had separated them. Even though the Red Cross had located them earlier, she didn't dare go back to see them for fear that the Communist government in place would prevent her from leaving the country. With seven kids at home, it was too great a risk. Finally she was given permission to return without restriction, and she went to visit for the first time since she was twelve, accompanied by my oldest sister, Cuky. During that visit, my grandmother died.

Having always had a fascination with Romania, where my mother was born, and knowing that eventually my mother found her family after the war, I wanted to know who they were. I asked her if she would take me to meet her brothers and sisters if I bought my own ticket. Impressed with my ambition and curiosity, she agreed. "If you buy the ticket, we'll go."

I worked two jobs after school, one in an ice-cream parlor and one in a gift shop. It took me nine months, but I managed to save $817 for a round-trip Denver–Bucharest ticket. We left on October 17, 1976. At the last minute my sister Cuky, a flight attendant, also joined us.

Arriving in Bucharest was like arriving on the moon for me. Everything was so different from Denver, and because it was so different my intuition was working overtime. One morning I woke up and said to my mother, "I have a strong feeling we'll meet your godmother, Mom. I think I dreamt it." At the time I didn't even know my mom had a godmother! My mother said, "Sonia, my godmother must be dead. She's got to be over ninety for sure."

Later that day my uncle took us for a drive, stopping at the graveyard where my grandparents were buried. After visiting their graves, we left in a somber mood. My uncle Costel, a bright and exuberant person, reached over and touched my mom's elbow. "Now, surprise!" he said in his very basic English.

He led us down the road about two hundred yards to a spot where a very, very old lady was sitting on a bench. My uncle said something to my mother in Romanian, and she threw up her arms in shock. She turned to me and said in astonishment, "My God, Sonia, you were right! This is my godmother."

A strange feeling of awe and satisfaction flushed over me. It was one of the most important affirming moments of my life.

Sometimes people tell me, "Travel is great, but what if you can't travel? What if you don't have money or time to get away?" I maintain that you can always find ways to have an adventure if you really want to. An overnight camping trip would be a start, or a day trip to a neighboring city. Use your imagination. It begins there. And if you're truly unable to get away, there are other imaginative ways to travel with your kids.

ADVENTURING AT HOME

My friend Shenoa, who has raised a very intuitive and creative son, says, "When I was a young single mother in New York, working paycheck to paycheck, one thing Adam and I always did was have dinner in a foreign country every Sunday. First we'd choose a country, and then I'd prepare a meal from that country. His assignment was to learn what he could about the country. During the week I'd go to the store and he'd go to the encyclopedia, and on Sunday we'd meet at the dinner table. By the time he moved out we'd been all over the world together, and each trip was only the price of dinner for two."

In Adam's day the encyclopedia was the source of his adventures. Now, any kid with a computer can go even further. A sense of adventure fosters curiosity, which is an essential fuel for the engine of intuition.

Travel and adventure take on even greater importance as more kids grow up in sequestered and isolated suburban communities, where a homogenized culture filters out variety. If every one of the families your children are exposed to have essentially the same lifestyle, the same background, the same skin color, the same values and opinions—your children's perspective will become biased and narrow. Just remember that an essential quality needed to stimulate intuitive muscles is variety.

Be creative in introducing your kids to a love of adventure and discovery. We live in a fascinating and fantastic world. My teacher Dr. Tully always said that intuition works best on a foundation of knowledge. The more you know of people and of the world, the greater the foundation of knowledge you draw upon.

USING CREATIVE INCENTIVE

When you engage a child's interest and give him an incentive, his intuition will kick in. My teacher Charlie Goodman taught me that intuition works a little differently for everyone. "Intuition follows your natural interest, and everyone's interests are different," he said. "Where your interest is, your intuition is right behind."

Twenty years ago my husband Patrick's friend Phil was living with his wife and their five-year-old son, Joey, in their old farmhouse in Iowa. It was Christmastime, and Joey kept pestering Phil about his presents. Two days before Christmas Phil finally said to Joey, "If you can find your presents, then you can open them!"

This set Joey free. He looked high, low, and everywhere, but all he came up with were two very old boxes of Tide laundry soap that he had found in the basement. One was open, the soap crusted over, but the other appeared intact. Phil threw away the open box and tossed the sealed one in the laundry basket.

The next day the three of them went to the Laundromat to wash clothes for Christmas. Phil opened the old box of Tide, teasing Joey that this was his Christmas present. As he poured the soap into the machine, a big wad of pre–Civil War silver certificate dollar bills, stuck together into a solid brick, came tumbling out. Apparently someone had hidden these bills in the box and carefully resealed it.

All three stood with their mouths hanging open. What a find on Christmas Eve! They sat impatiently waiting for their laundry to finish, stuffed it still wet into bags straight from the washer, and raced home with their treasure. After thinking it over, they contacted an attorney to ask what to do. After investigating the matter, a judge ruled that since they had bought the house including anything left there, the money was theirs free and clear! They sent the bills to the U.S. Treasury, which promptly returned a check for $35,515. Joey still talks about finding that box. He's sure a Christmas angel showed him where it was.

Kids love to be intuitively challenged, especially if they have an incentive. Here's another example of intuition following genuine interest and enthusiasm.

Two months ago we lost our good Nikon camera. Patrick, the girls, and I looked everywhere, even "Wondering" to the best of our ability, but after searching in every nook and cranny, we finally gave up. Throwing in the towel at dinner one evening, I suggested to Patrick that maybe it was for the best. Perhaps it was the Universe's way of telling us to retire the old thing. It was fifteen years old, and even though Patrick had a great affection for the camera, which had accompanied him around the world, I had secretly wanted to buy a new one for some time. Reluctantly Patrick agreed.

Sonia listened closely and after a moment said, "Dad, since you're buying a new camera, if I find the old one, can I have it? After all, if you're getting a new one, you won't need it, right?"

Patrick answered, "Sure, Wooze, if you can find it, it's yours."

"Will you teach me to use it if I find it?" she persisted.

"Sure. I'd be happy to."

For several days after that conversation I overheard Sonia asking herself, "I wonder where that camera is?" One day as she was riding in the backseat of the car on the way home from school she said, "I hope I find the camera, Mom. I really want it."

The very next day I had to go to the post office and took Sonia along with me. Annoyed at having to go, she flopped down in the backseat of the car, pouting.

Just as I was shutting the car door behind me I heard Sonia say, "What's this?" This caught my attention, and I turned around to look in the car as she was pulling out a brown plastic bag from under the seat on the driver's side. I watched her sit up, open the bag, and scream. She flung open the car door and yelled, "Mom, guess what! I found the camera! I found it!"

"Well, it's yours, Sonia," I said, very impressed with her find. "Congratulations!"

She was beaming. By the time we got home her father had arrived home, too. "Dad, Dad, I found the camera!" she squealed.

Patrick was shocked. She kept repeating, "I *really* wanted that camera! That's why I found it." Then suddenly she sobered up. "Dad, don't worry. I'll let you borrow it anytime until you can afford one of your own."

You can engage your children's intuition very easily if you can discern where their real interests lie, but the key is *their* real interests—not yours. What does your child really care about?

GIVE THEM A VOTE

Yet another way to exercise your children's intuitive muscles is to give them a vote on what's happening in their lives. Wherever you can allow their input, ask for it. Whether it's decorating their room, dressing themselves, or choosing after-school activities, let them choose what they like. Don't force your children to silently acquiesce to your ideas of who they are. And don't put them in the position of making you look good. It's *their* childhood. Let them have it! Remember, good, bad, or otherwise, your own is over. You can recapture the child in you by playing with them, but don't squash the child in *them* by taking away all the fun.

Let them choose. Let them express preferences. Allow them to have an opinion and to speak without being censored. This does not imply anarchy. Of course you should have family rules that establish respect, responsibility, and cooperation. But those rules do not have to squash your children's individuality. In fact, when it comes to rules, invite your children to participate in setting those rules.

Give them practice at making decisions. After all, making better decisions is the point of enhancing your intuition. Where decisions govern safety and protection, of course you must be in charge, but where you can let them decide on matters without endangering them, hand over the reins. Invite their input on as many aspects of their life as is appropriate for their age. When they run to you for answers, first ask how they would solve the problem. When they express desires, ask them first how they would try to meet them. When they come to you squabbling, ask them to work it out. As much as is reasonable, give them the incentive to find their own way. You'd be surprised what a little creative incentive can do for a kid's intuition.

HANG A BRIGHT IDEA BOARD

Another terrific way to encourage intuition and creativity in the family is to create a bright idea board, a bulletin board put up exclusively for the purpose of expressing and sharing bright ideas. You can hang the bright idea board in the kitchen or family room or wherever all family members will have access to it. Invite them to write down all inspirations, intuitive insights, gut feelings, and bright ideas and post them on the bright idea board as they come up. Establish creative sanctity around this idea center, and insist that all ideas contributed will be considered and none will be ridiculed.

During family meals or in the family meeting if you are having one, you can review and discuss these bright ideas. Use the suggestions on the board to fuel the fires of family brainstorming. It's fun and extremely productive and encourages creative and intuitive thinking.

RESPECT THEIR STYLE

Another opportunity for the kind of creative expression that allows children to find and follow their own truth is in being free to choose their own style and taste in clothing. As any mother will admit, having a new baby to dress up can be a lot of fun. It's like playing with dolls all over again, only this time they're real!

It can be very easy to forget that our children are not our playthings, to be dressed up, molded, and forced to comply with our ideas of who they are. They are individuals with their own ideas and creative needs, a fact I was reminded of quite pointedly by Sonia at age three.

One of my favorite pleasures in life is a *great* pair of shoes, and this affection for great shoes spilled over into wanting them for Sonia and Sabrina as well. A few years ago, when I worked for an airline and traveled frequently to Europe, I discovered that European baby shoes are simply the best in the world. My girls had the snappiest, happiest feet this side of the Atlantic all through toddlerhood. The girls themselves were oblivious of their uptown shoes, but it was great fun for me.

One day I put Sonia into a magnificent pair of magenta-and-turquoise suede high-top lace-up boots that I had purchased in Italy, only to find her twenty minutes later in the backyard, slopping through mud puddles.

"Sonia, get out of the puddle this minute!" I yelled from the kitchen window, disgusted that *my* new shoes were now hopelessly stained.

She looked up at me, totally confused. "Why, Mommy?"

"Because you're ruining your new shoes!"

Annoyed, Sonia stomped out of the puddle and came into the house.

"Ah, Sonia, just look at these shoes! They're ruined," I lamented, peeling them off her feet.

"Mom," she answered, just as disgusted with me as I was with her, "next time please buy them in *your* size, okay?"

Her comment stopped me cold. She was so right, I had to laugh. It was true—I had bought those shoes for myself. I didn't for one second ever think to take Sonia's personality into consideration when I bought them. Sonia was no prima donna. She was a rough-and-tumble, tree-climbing, bike-riding, sandbox-playing kind of girl. Those shoes were ridiculous for her. What she needed was a good pair of canvas shoes or rubber boots. All my projections of what I liked were cramping her style, and she let me know it in no uncertain terms.

Our conversation taught me a very important lesson in respecting who my children are. Choosing clothing, like all else that is sensual, is part of a child's unique creativity. Ever since that episode I have made a genuine effort to let my children make their own choices of clothing whenever practical. Almost invariably, both Sonia and Sabrina choose something other than what I would have selected. Yet when they do choose their clothes, they wear them to death. It's both supportive to their sense of individuality and practical for our budget!

Kids need to be free to be creative, and that definitely includes having a vote in how to dress, as well as having the freedom to play, get dirty, and *be a kid*! Apart from clothing that obviously may create problems, like gang attire or shorts in a snowstorm, recognize that choosing their own clothes is part of children's personal creative expression: appreciate your child's sense of style!

LIGHTEN UP

No matter what methods you use to engage your children's intuition, the most important aspect is your attitude. If you are a perfectionist, a control freak, or a drama queen, chances are you will have little success in creating an atmosphere of wonder and discovery, the necessary playground for young intuitives.

One of my own hobbies is collecting and studying the history of the tarot. In all tarot decks, which are based on a pictorial book from the Middle Ages designed to teach mastery of life, the very first card is the Fool, a lighthearted time traveler ready to descend to planet Earth to have a worldly experience. In his hand is a rose, representing desire. On his back he carries a satchel full of his talents. At his feet is a little white dog representing his intellect, companion to his soul. Above all, he has lightness of foot.

This card tells us to travel lightly. We all have to play the Fool from time to time in life. We need first to laugh at our mistakes before we can learn from them. Laughter brings distance, perception, and sometimes insight. It also reminds us that who we are (spiritual beings, time travelers here on earth to create) and what we do (make mistakes) are not the same thing. It keeps our self-worth intact as it emphasizes the need to look foolish at times to gain discovery.

If you as a parent laugh easily and live light of heart, your children will feel safe and joyful in discovering life. Have you ever heard them laugh over nothing? Over goofing up? Over being the fool? Left to their own natural impulses, children laugh and laugh. They learn to stop laughing only if no one else in the house laughs with them. Be honest and easygoing enough to admit your errors to them. Say "I'm sorry" or "I'm tired" or "I need space" or "Give me a moment" when you need to. Let your needs be met as democratically as possible. Don't be a martyr, a boss, a victim, or a drag. Lighten up! Play with them. Intuition is a resonating energy. If they use it, so will you. If you use it, so will they.

Tools FOR CREATING A SENSE OF WONDER AND DISCOVERY

Have your children "wonder"
> who is calling when the phone rings.
> where you'll find a parking space.
> when the elevator will come.
> when the teacher will give a pop quiz.
> who will win the school football game.
> what science project to do for an assignment.
> where are my books . . . my shoes.

Let a sense of adventure take you to
> a new part of town.
> a new cultural arts performance.
> the study of another race.
> eating a new type of food.
> a new city or country.
> exploring another religion.
> inviting a new person to dinner.

Give your children a vote on
    whom to be friends with.
    what vegetable to eat for dinner.
    what to study in school.
    how to spend summer vacation.
    where to go for dinner.

Let your children choose
    what to wear.
    how to decorate their rooms.
    how to wear their hair.
    what music to listen to.
    their preferences without insult or judgment from you.

Together, try
    laughing.
    singing.
    telling jokes.
    doing new things.
    making mistakes without censure.
    being *very* curious.
    acting silly and playing the fool.

Reflections

1. Do you allow your own sense of wonder to come into play? How?

_____

_____

_____

2. Are you beginning to notice the subtle energy around you?

_____

_____

_____

3. Have you introduced the I Wonder game to your children? What happened?

_____

_____

_____

4. Are you creating a sense of fun and delight when you play the game? When?

_____

_____

_____

5. What are some of the discoveries playing I Wonder has introduced?

_____

_____

_____

6. Where have you adventured with your children lately?

_____

_____

_____

7. Are you encouraging your children to flex their intuitive muscles? How?

_____

_____

_____

8. Is there any room for spontaneity in your family life? Give a few examples.

_____

_____

_____

REMINDERS
Are you:
    Creating your own language of spirit?
    Remembering to clear your aura and those of your kids?
    Being respectful of all vibes, however inconvenient or unpleasant?
    Being playful, having adventures?

✳ TEN

Asking for Guidance

One of the most exciting things you will discover when actively calling upon intuition is that you and your children are infinitely supported in your goal. The Universe is ready, willing, and able to assist you and guide you just for the asking. But before divine support can assist you, you need to *ask* the Universe for help and guidance.

Asking for intuitive guidance is a habit your children will learn from you. Let them know early on that they are children of the Universe and that the Universe is watching over them, wanting them to succeed in life. Kids respond well to the knowledge that the Universe is on their side and that they can tap into Divine support simply by asking.

The first question kids ask me when I tell them that the Universe *wants* to help them is, "What things can I ask for help on?" To which I answer, "Everything—except how to cheat." I explain that the Universe cares for them so much that it provides them with love, protection, safety, inspiration, ideas, solutions, and everything else they need to grow and thrive in life. One child, Cheryl, asked me if the Universe would do her homework for her.

I answered, "No, it won't do your homework, but it will help *you* do your homework."

"Rats!" Cheryl said, shrugging. "Oh well, at least it's something."

The Universe takes on a friendly, kind, and loving countenance for kids when they become aware that Divine energy is behind them. And as they get older, in a world where guns, violence, alcohol, and drugs are often just as much a part of their lives as dances and baseball, it's very comforting to them to know that they have extra help available.

My mother introduced me early on to the practice of asking for help from the Universe. Whenever I had a problem, whether it was finding my shoes or struggling because my best friend was not speaking to me, I was taught to ask for help and assistance. One way I did this was by playing a game my mother taught me called Fishing for Solutions. In this game I focused on my heart and then cast my mind into the Universe like a fishing line and asked the Universe to catch a solution to my problem for me.

Once I argued with my mom about whether or not this would work.

"Sure it will, Sonia. Wherever there is a problem there is always a solution. In fact, God gives us problems just so we can enjoy the creativity and satisfaction of catching a solution," she said. "That's the fun of life!"

When I first began casting for a solution, I'd wait only a moment or two before becoming impatient. "Mom," I'd say, "this is dumb. I am *not* catching anything."

To which she would answer, "Be patient, Sonia. Fishing for a solution is no different from fishing for fish. It takes time. A solution won't come if you keep pulling on the line. Just relax and let your creative hook sit out there in the Universe for a while, and go do something else. When the solution comes it'll pull on your awareness and you can draw it in."

So I'd try again. I'd cast my problem out to the Universe and then . . . forget about it.

I remember very clearly when I caught my first solution. I had a big problem with a new girl named Lillian who had just entered my third-grade class. I knew about Lillian, who lived in the neighborhood. She was very big and very mean. For some reason on her first day at our school, Lillian decided she didn't like me, but she did like my two best friends, Susie and Darlene. In no time my friends had dropped me. I was very hurt by this rejection and betrayal, and for the first time in my life I was physically frightened. Lillian often boasted of fighting, and I was afraid she'd actually beat me up.

I asked my mom for advice about Lillian, and after a moment of reflection she said, "Hmmm. I'm not sure what to do, but I do have a suggestion. Why don't you ask your spirit to fish for a solution to this one."

I remember being annoyed with this idea because I felt as though she were using it as a way to dismiss me, but she stopped me in midcomplaint when I accused her of doing nothing.

"Sonia," she interrupted, "asking the Universe for help is *not* 'doing nothing.' It's doing the smartest possible thing because it opens your mind to answers that are new. Now go to your room and do your homework. Something will bite while you work. I'm sure of it."

Not getting the instant satisfaction I wanted, I went to my room in a snit, but diving into my homework calmed me down. I'm not exactly sure when I felt a pull on the "solution line," but I was somewhere in the middle of my geography book when suddenly an idea popped into my mind.

It occurred to me out of nowhere that Lillian was an only child. Both Darlene and Susie were also only children, and all three of them were girls whose parents were separated and whose dads were rarely around. Maybe she didn't like me because I had lots of brothers and sisters and a dad. Maybe she was jealous!

My fishing line pulled harder. It told me to invite Lillian to go swimming with my family at the Celebrity Lanes swimming pool on Sunday night, which was our weekly family ritual. It seemed odd, since Lillian hated me, but intuition insisted.

I ran to my mom's sewing room. "Guess what, Mom! I think I caught a solution! Maybe I should invite Lillian swimming with our family on Sunday. What do you think?"

My mom thought for a moment and said, "That's an interesting idea, Sonia. Why not? Give it a try."

When I called Lillian she was surprised to receive an invitation from *me*. After I asked her to join us for the evening, there was a long silence on the other end of the line. And then . . . to my great relief she said, "Okay, but I have to ask my mom first. I'll call you back and tell you whether I can go or not when she gets home."

After dinner Lillian called back to say yes, she could come with us, and she showed up on Sunday evening with her bathing suit. She jumped in the car with the seven of us kids and my dad (no seat belts in those days), and off we went. In the car Lillian was so meek and mild that I didn't even recognize her, but at the pool she warmed up and dropped her defenses.

We had a wonderful time. We jumped off the deep end, slid down the slide, played shark, and laughed all the way home. She wasn't mean or angry at all that evening, and from that night on Lillian and I were friends. Soon we were playing with Darlene and Susie, who made up with me, and things settled back to normal. I always attributed that friendship to Fishing for Solutions.

You can teach your kids to fish for a solution whenever they are stuck. Suggest to them that their awareness is like a creative fishing line that they can cast into the Universal Sea of ideas and solutions. All they must do is focus on their heart, ask for guidance, cast their awareness into the Universe, and wait for a "catch." You can pretend to cast the line with very young kids of three, four, five, even six—they love this; with older ones, you can ask them to do it mentally. Either way works. Fishing doesn't require anything more than the intention to reel in a solution and the receptivity to receive one. Solutions exist and are there for those who seek them. My teacher Charlie Goodman once told me that problems and solutions go together, and where there is one there is the other, attracted to each other like magnets.

When I taught my daughter Sonia at age six to fish for a solution, she asked me, "What do we use for bait?"

I answered, "Why, the problem itself, of course. Solutions *love* to gobble up problems!" She seemed satisfied.

One thing I've noticed in rushed parents these days (myself included) is that rather than having the patience or taking the time to encourage our children to fish for solutions to problems, we prefer to just hand them answers. After all, it saves us time and may be very easy. But giving answers discourages creative thinking and takes away the potential joy a child will experience in discovering them on his own. And we may give answers that aren't the best ones for our children.

My spiritual teachers *never* gave me solutions, only ways of discovering them on my own. If I ever needed an answer or guidance, I had to *work* for it. For example, I'd often talk to Charlie about school and friendship. Never being terribly popular, I often felt like an ugly duckling in school and was very self-conscious most of the time. I would ask Charlie why the girls in school didn't like me or what I could do to change that, but he never answered me directly. Instead he'd answer, "That's a very good question, Sonia. Better ask spirit for guidance on that one!"

As frustrating as it was, his answer did teach me to ask for guidance, which to my amazement eventually did arrive by way of insight, inspiration, and "pops" of understanding from time to time. My guidance told me that my lack of popularity in school had everything to do with my interests. Once my guidance said to me, "You are simply a deep-sea diver in a crowd of water-skiers." That made me laugh and helped me keep my spirits up as I began to look for other "deep-sea divers."

ASKING FOR HELP

Fishing for Solutions was only one way to get spiritual guidance in our house. My mother also had an ongoing direct dialogue with spirit all the time, conversing openly with spirit as easily as she conversed with us. It was not at all unusual for my mom to turn to her heart and ask, usually out loud, for the Universe not only to guide her, but to actually help her accomplish what she needed to accomplish in every way. If she needed help on one of her art projects, such as her painting, sewing, or photography, she would summon spirit to get on the job with her. She wasn't spacey or weird about it. She was direct, simple, and to the point.

After taking a home study course on photography for two years and graduating with honors, my mother wanted to open a studio in our basement. While setting it up, she spent more money than my dad wanted her to, and he got very cranky about it.

"I hope this hobby of yours doesn't continue to cost so much. We can't afford too much more!" he commented one day, which made my mom quite mad.

"You are insulting!" she retorted, extremely irritated with his lack of enthusiasm. "This is *not* a hobby, I'll have you know! I am a professional! I'll pay for this studio with my own money, you'll see. *Mark my words.*" (This was a favorite expression.)

That night as I sat with her in the darkroom while she developed the photos she had taken earlier of us kids, she took my hand and said, "Sonia, we need to ask spirit to send me some work. Lots of it, in fact—and fast." Then she turned to me and said, "Let's ask spirit to bring me lots and lots of work and money so your father will relax!"

"Okay," I said as I stared at her closed eyes through the green glow of the darkroom light. "I'll ask for help, too." Quietly I watched her pray for assistance. Then I closed my eyes and said to myself, "Divine Spirit, my mom needs lots and lots of work so Dad will stop complaining about the cost of her studio. Will you help her, please?"

After a moment my mother squeezed my hand and said, "Okay. I feel spirit heard us, and I'm sure spirit will get busy. Now let it go. Spirit is on the job, so we can relax." It was as though that squeeze of my hand were a signal to trust and let spirit do the work. So I did.

Less than a week later I came home from school with my brothers and sisters to find my mother rushing around frantically straightening up the house. "Quick, help me clean up," she said to us. "We're having company any minute, and I want the place to look good!"

We dropped our books and began dashing around, plumping pillows and wielding the vacuum. "Who's coming?" I asked, gathering the morning newspaper off the couch.

She stopped and smiled. "You'll never believe it, Sonia. Your entire school—kids, teachers, and all—will be here soon, beginning with the principal."

"Why?" I asked incredulously. "What for?"

"Because I got a call today from Sister Mary Canisius, asking me if I would be interested in taking the school photos—from the first grade to the seniors in high school, plus the teachers—starting this evening! It seems the regular studio they use was overbooked this year and they couldn't begin taking photos for another two months. Sister didn't want to wait, so she asked me to do it instead! Can you believe it?"

"Wow, Mom, I guess spirit really took us seriously when we asked for *lots* of work the other night."

"It sure did," my mom answered. "Now, let's get finished."

For the next two weeks the students from my school filed, grade by grade, through our front door and down to her basement studio one at a time. My mom did such a good job photographing each child that almost every parent ordered one of her photos. From that job she was asked to do family portraits, weddings, and business portraits. Her business virtually exploded overnight.

I was amazed at how generous and speedy the Universe was in putting my mom into business. So was my dad. All she had to do was ask—and, of course, *expect* to receive what she asked for—and she was on her way.

PRAYER

The most direct way to encourage your children to ask for help is to teach them to pray. Most kids like to pray once they learn how and will do it naturally in some form or another anyway. My sister Cuky once told me a story about my nephew concerning prayer.

Cuky was pregnant at the time, and she and her son Sean were walking hand in hand to the park. Halfway there, Sean looked up at his pregnant mother's belly and said, "Mom, there's just one thing I've *got* to know."

Expecting him to ask about the baby and how it got into her belly, Cuky braced herself for an explanation. "Yes, Sean? What do you have to know?"

He paused, thinking about it for another minute. "Well," he said thoughtfully, "just what the heck is Mrs. God's name, anyway? I have to ask her for something, and I don't know what to call her!"

Very few people I've encountered pray in a productive way. I've observed that while people do pray, they do not release their prayers into the heart of the Universe with any confidence that the Universe will work on their requests. Instead they continue to hold on to their worries with a viselike grip.

The key to successful prayer is learning to release the prayers to God. Once you have prayed, release the problem. Whenever my mom prayed with us, we always ended our prayers with a squeeze of her hand and the message to let it go. "It's done. Now let's relax!" By doing this, we infused our prayers with faith. That squeeze of the hand seemed to be the indefinable something that transformed them from wishful thinking and fearful whining into a powerful and profound sense of conviction. When the hand was squeezed, the Universe was on the job!

Praying with kids can be done in any way you like. Prayers can be said in a formal way, in the morning or at night. They can be said on your knees, at the table, in bed. Or kids can be taught to be in a state of constant prayer, asking for help as the need arises, all day long. The best way to teach children to pray is to have them watch you pray or, better yet, to have them pray with you. Example is the best teacher.

I have a friend, Wendy, whose grandfather was a faith healer and prayed all the time, out loud. She remembers many times when she and her four siblings would be riding in the car with Grandpa, indulging in their usual squabbles, and Grandpa would burst out in prayer. "Dear God, we pray to Thee to *heal* all the temperamentalness of someone in this car! We won't say who it is, so as *not* to embarrass anyone, but he or she *knows* who they are. Amen."

Laughing, Wendy recalled, "Every time Grandpa said this prayer out loud we'd all get very quiet. After all, we didn't know what 'temperamentalness' meant, but it didn't sound very good, and besides, we didn't want to be embarrassed by admitting to being the guilty one. Corny or not, his prayers always worked. And because they've worked for him I've prayed it myself to this day, especially when I'm around someone causing trouble. And it works as well for me as it did for him. Especially if I pray out loud." She smiled.

My own mother's prayer style was praying anytime, anywhere, asking for whatever the situation required, from finding her keys to sending healing energy to a sick friend. All it required was a bowed head, closed eyes, and inward reflection. Sometimes she prayed out loud, sometimes not.

My best friend Suzanne's mother also prayed, but her praying style was more formal. She preferred to kneel down and say rosaries in the morning. My friend Lu Ann's mother created a sacred atmosphere for prayer, enlisting the aid of holy water and candles. Another friend's mother plays religious music, usually Gregorian chants, when she wants to pray.

Whatever approach you take, the truth is that you can choose how you pray. After all, prayer is really having a private chat with God. Any way is valid if you are sincere. Whether you pray spontaneously or with a more ritualized approach depends upon your temperament, the situation, and what feels right for you at that moment.

GRATITUDE AS PRAYER

One of the most powerful ways to pray is to practice gratitude. Gratitude affects our consciousness the way windshield wipers affect a windshield in a blizzard. It clears away confusion and helps us see the world more clearly.

Practicing gratitude as a form of prayer is very easy and is immediately rewarding. All you need to do is acknowledge and thank the Universe for all your blessings, whether they are good health, family, friends, or simply being alive. I personally keep a gratitude journal. As a family we keep a gratitude bulletin board in the kitchen on which we post photos of happy experiences and appreciative acknowledgments for the things we have received. It's amazing to realize just how much we all have to be grateful for once we begin to notice.

Practicing gratitude instantly lightens the heart and helps us remember how much we are loved and supported by the Universe. Whenever my children or I are restless, irritable, anxious, bored, uneasy, or fearful, I suggest we think of as many things as possible to be grateful for to change the energy. We list our blessings one at a time, trying to name at least ten things. Every time we do this our fear subsides and our hearts and intuition open.

Practicing gratitude keeps a child's awareness focused on the abundance, support, and love that the Universe has for him. It focuses his heart and awareness on receiving all that is available to him and reminds him to remain in a state of receptivity and peace.

These are only some ways to pray. You may have an entirely different way. Some people chant their prayer. Some pray on beads or rosaries. Some say prayers silently. Others pray in groups. Some sing their prayers. Some have an ongoing dialogue with God. Some meditate on prayer. All ways to pray are valid.

Your prayer style is very personal, and all styles are valid. Use whatever approach and tradition you prefer in asking for divine help, and know that Divine Spirit, God, is love and that the Universe loves you completely and unconditionally, as you are, faults and all. Whether praying by yourself or with your child, realize that the Universe *wants* to help, would *love* to help. But first you must ask.

The great teacher Jesus Christ taught the importance of prayer when he was questioned about miracles. "Of myself I do nothing," he said. "It is my Father in Heaven who works through me." Or as the saying goes, "If God is with you, then who can be against you? After all, there is no power greater than God."

911 MIRACLE BOX

One of the most delightful ways to ask the Universe for support was shown to me by my friend Lu Ann Glatzmaier. When I was fourteen Lu Ann and I became friends. My mother, to whom she had come for lessons, first introduced me to her, and ours has been a parallel path from the beginning. Like me, she showed unusual intuitive abilities at an early age, and like me, she has followed the healer's path. Lu showed me a unique way to ask for help by making what she called an alchemy box. Together, over several sessions, we decorated shoeboxes inside and out with tissue paper, stickers, and pieces of paper with affirmations, spiritual symbols, and images of angels. Afterward we each placed all our written special requests and prayers in our box, as a symbolic act of surrendering our requests in faith, so that the Universe could work on them. To my amazement and delight, every time I placed a request in my box it eventually was answered. Other names for this hand-decorated box are wish box, prayer box, angel box—even 911 Miracle Box! I call it an alchemy box, because alchemy means transmutation or change.

Whatever you call it, making an alchemy box brings out the kid in everyone. It has been the birthday party activity of choice for both Sonia and Sabrina because, they say, "Even though we have alchemy boxes, we want our friends to have them, too. Every kid needs one!"

My daughter Sonia has her alchemy box covered with stickers and pictures of animals and fish cut out of magazines because she is crazy about them. She has blue tissue on the inside with stickers of dolphins and fish, and brown and green tissue paper on the outside with images of horses, lions, cats, dogs, and elephants.

The themes for Sabrina's box are more mythic and celestial. Hers is covered in blue tissue paper with moons, stars, and pictures of suns, angels, saints, rainbows, and comets. On the inside it's covered with hearts.

Making these boxes with the girls was a family affair. We spent over two weeks preparing our materials. We chose boxes from our closets. We bought tissue. We pored over *National Geographic* magazines and cut out pictures. We went to the stationery store for stickers. Finally, we visited an arts and crafts store for acrylic, sprinkles, and glue. The process was fun and created a sense of anticipation.

The day finally came when we all sat at the kitchen table and began to decorate and assemble our boxes, all the while talking about the elements we especially loved. We discussed what we chose to decorate our boxes with and why. When we were finished we sprayed them with clear acrylic to protect them. We laughed and had a delightfully creative day, preparing a place to keep our prayers and requests safe while the Universe worked on them.

When the boxes were finished we each placed a prayer inside. Then we all held hands, Patrick, Sabrina, Sonia, and I, and asked spirit to work on our prayers for us and to bless our miracle boxes and ourselves.

Over the years we have begun a New Year's Eve ritual with our boxes. On that night we pull out our boxes and place in them our wishes and prayers for the New Year. On New Year's Day we open the boxes again and read our list from the year before. Every time we do this we laugh and cheer at how many special prayers were answered.

Making an alchemy box really captures a child's imagination and teaches her, through creativity, art, and invention, how to surrender prayers to the Universe and *allow* the Universe to work on the job. Once a child has created an alchemy box, you can suggest that she write on a piece of paper all special requests and spiritual emergencies she may have at any time, for any reason. The very act of doing this helps a child focus on her needs, actually ask spirit for help, and then release the request in faith. It also teaches the child patience in keeping "hands off" her worries and allowing the Universe to work on her behalf.

An alchemy box combines creativity with an open heart and a receptive mind. It establishes a frame of mind in your child that connects him to their Source. The combination of art and prayer puts your child in a position to access, through his own imagination and creativity, all the love, guidance, and protection of the Universe.

When we feel alone, life is tough. It is so much kinder and easier for your child when he knows the Universe is with him.

Tool MAKING YOUR OWN ALCHEMY BOX

Supply list:
   A shoebox
   Colored tissue paper
   Glue stick
   Stickers of inspiring images
   Glitter
   Holy cards
   Affirmations
   Photos

Pictures of your heart's desires
Acrylic spray

Gather your supplies together over a period of several weeks. Plan in advance a time to assemble your boxes. As you work, play inspirational and uplifting music. This is also a wonderful activity for a children's party. Everyone young and old needs an alchemy box for special requests. Make the time to create one, and let it begin to work for you.

Tool FISHING FOR SOLUTIONS

As a family, get into the habit of fishing for solutions together. Whenever a family member has a quandary, dilemma, problem, or issues, invite everyone in the family to cast their creative lines into the Universe and reel in support, inspiration, answers, and direction to help them. Reel in everything that comes up. Don't censor a thing. If it doesn't work, you can always throw it back. The more the family works together on this technique, the more delightful and creative the outcome.

Tool PRAY TOGETHER

The most powerful prayers are those prayed with the full awareness of being a beloved child of God. Prayers prayed with a deep sense that the Universe wants to help you, guide you, support you, delight you, and love you unconditionally are the prayers most quickly and satisfactorily answered. Prayers prayed with others who share this knowledge are yet even more powerful.

Create a time when you can pray as a family. This can be at dinner-time or bedtime or after family meeting time. It is also important to encourage your family to ask each other to pray with and for them whenever they are feeling upset or concerned or need a little extra help.

As Jesus said, "Whenever two or more are gathered in my name, I will be there also."

Reflections

1. Have you taught your children how to fish for solutions? Have they tried? When?

_____

_____

_____

2. Are they getting results?

_____

_____

_____

3. Have you "fished" as a family? Catch anything interesting?

_____

_____

_____

4. Do you pray? When?

_____

_____

_____

5. Do you pray with your children? When?

_____

_____

_____

6. Do you ask each other to help you pray for special intentions?

_____

_____

_____

7. Do your children pray on their own? How?

_____

_____

_____

REMINDERS

Are you:

    Being playful, having adventures?

    Using your artistic talents?

    Remembering to ask for help?

    Aware that the Universe loves you and wants to help?

ELEVEN

Contemplation and Art

Creating the right atmosphere for awakening intuition is one part of the equation for living an intuitive life. Quieting ourselves enough to hear our spirit speak is the other. We have to tune out the distractions of the world from time to time to connect with the subtle beauty and expression of our souls. Though it may take an effort on the part of a pressured adult to make time for inward reflection and creative expression, children fall into such instinctive connections with the soul naturally in two distinct and separate ways.

The first is when they enter into the natural trance of quiet play and reverie. It might occur when they are building blocks, swinging on a swing set, or digging in the dirt. Or it may occur when they daydream in the car or stare into space at the dinner table. No matter what the way, all children drift automatically into their own quiet healing space when they need to rest and connect with their soul, if left to do so freely and without judgment or interference from others.

The second way children connect with their spirit is through the expression of art. Whether in passionate finger-painting sessions, banging on drums or piano keys, or intensely writing his first original fiction story, a child's artistic expression is actually his *soul* expression. If contemplation is our reaching for our soul, creative and artistic expression is the soul's reaching for us. No wonder it is such a beloved activity of children, especially young children, worldwide. It is their opportunity to make contact with and express their most genuine and authentic being.

Contemplation and art are the two most direct avenues for a child to get in touch with his creative essence and his intuition, or "inner teacher." Both exercises should be recognized for their essentially soul-healing importance and should be encouraged and fully supported by you.

First let's look at the importance of quiet time as a way for a child to connect with his spirit. At first glance it may seem to you that your active and sometimes even hyperactive child may never seek quiet time unless you enforce it. It is my experience with kids, however, that this is most likely an inaccurate observation. I encourage all parents to practice an exercise in awareness in noticing how their children naturally do seek to connect with their spirits, on their own time and in their own way. Perhaps it is they who can be your teacher now.

A client named Linda called me to tell me about her nephew Paul, who had just visited her for the weekend. She said that she lived in a high-rise building with a rooftop pool, and she decided that going to the pool would be a fun thing for them to do together. When they got to the pool Linda said to Paul, "You go ahead and swim. I'm just going to sit by the side and read awhile. Let me know when you're ready to go."

Paul jumped into the water, and Linda settled in with her book. A good while passed, and she suddenly noticed that it was very quiet. She looked over to the pool and saw Paul floating on a raft with his eyes half-closed, staring into the water as if in a trance. Surprised to find him in such a tranquil state, she watched him for a while. He lay there motionless for another ten full minutes, and then slowly he blinked, stretched, looked over at her, and smiled.

"Paul, what were you doing?" Linda asked.

Calmly he said, "Oh, just meditating."

Linda was surprised, to say the least. She could hardly imagine that anyone in Paul's family, including her sister, would be interested in such activities, let alone teach him how.

"Meditating? Whoever told you about meditation?"

"I don't know," Paul replied. "I just know about it, and I do it all the time. I get good ideas when I do!"

Linda was impressed with Paul's natural and easy ability to do what she had been struggling unsuccessfully to experience for years. Like Paul, your children also have a natural "zoning out" technique or two that you can discover if you pay attention. Whatever it is, recognize it as their way of tuning inward and refreshing their soul, even if only for a moment or two. Perhaps they do what Paul does and float in a pool. Or perhaps they soak in the tub. Or lay on their back in their bed and stare at the ceiling. Or doodle on a piece of paper. Or play in a sandbox. These zoning out behaviors relax their mind and thoughts and help them tune in to the voice of their soul. This is natural meditation, although kids would probably not call it that, or even want to, because it sounds so serious. So unkidlike!

Respect their daydreaming and let them have their reverie when they do slip into it. Avoid the tendency to shake them out of it. Though it appears as though they are not doing something, they are. They are becoming reenergized by their soul. When I think of contemplation and reverie, I am reminded of one of Dr. Tully's favorite sayings: "One of the most powerful things you can do at times is nothing!" When it comes to connecting quietly with one's spirit, he was absolutely right. When children come out of their quiet period, you can ask them how they feel. You can let them know that being quiet is a good way to hear intuition.

CONTEMPLATION SOOTHES THE SOUL

Travel is so important to our children, but it does involve a great deal of stress because everything is new, different, and often out of our control. For Sonia and Sabrina it means leaving the comfort of home, familiar surroundings, routines, and their friends, which isn't easy for them.

One day a while ago, we were driving in the rain, heading toward home after an extended stay away. Sabrina said quite spontaneously, "You know, Dad, when I have to sleep in places I've never been before, instead of getting scared, I just think of my favorite toy, and everything I like about it for as long as I can. Then I feel like I'm home and I go to sleep."

"Sabrina," I said, very impressed, "what a good idea. That's called meditating."

"Maybe, but I like calling it dreaming of my favorite toy instead." Then she continued to stare out the window, slipping back into her own private thoughts.

It reminded me once again of how kids naturally do the right thing and how we need to follow their good example. Sabrina's method was a great suggestion for teaching other kids how to tune inward and find peace. It's something they can do on a sleepover if they get nervous just before going to sleep. Or when they go on their first overnight camp. Or if they must go back and forth from Mom's house to Dad's house several times a month because of a divorce situation.

I really believe that there are many ways to achieve a state of inner calm and that sitting quietly is only one way. Sabrina tunes inward by focusing on something she loves. Paul did it while floating. Sonia likes daydreaming to quiet classical music as a way to tune inward. Her friend Madelyn calms herself by playing the piano. And, believe it or not, some kids even tune inward best while in motion. For example, my husband Patrick's favorite zoning out technique as a kid was skiing. He loved the quiet and beauty of the mountain and the concentration and focus it took for him to actually make it down the mountainside. Whenever he was ever in psychic overload, he grabbed his skis and headed for the hill. He still does. Another active mode of contemplation is swimming. Sonia is a true "fish" when it comes to swimming. Whenever we are on a beach she races straight for the water and stays in it for hours. Sometimes, if she has worn herself out from swimming, she'll relax in the shallow tide and allow the waves to wash over her, sitting like a Buddha with her eyes closed and her mind a million miles from earth. I call this active meditation. Active meditation is an equally valid way to tune inward and connect with one's soul, and in energetic children this approach is often a lot more practical for quieting emotions and thoughts and achieving a tranquil state than sitting is.

CONTEMPLATION IN DOING

One day Diane, a client, came to me for a reading because she was quite concerned over what she called "my nine-year-old banshee," her very hyperactive, athletic son, Lonnie, who could never give her a moment's peace. I could tell that he was indeed wearing her out with his restlessness, and she was at her wits' end.

"I have him in every sort of sport, Sonia. We live in a great neighborhood where he can play outside. We try to do things together as a family, but he's always so worked up and hyper, it's driving me mad. I can't seem to calm him down, and he's hard to be around. He's on Ritalin and it helps, but not much. Any ideas?"

I could tell from his personal vibration that he was indeed a very fiery kid with a lot of energy and had a lot of frustration in being unable to calm himself. My guides offered one suggestion, so I passed it along to Diane.

"Interest him in growing and caring for a garden," I said.

"What?"

"See if you can involve him in working in a garden," I repeated. "My intuition tells me that he is too fiery and needs more earth to quiet his nervous system."

"That's an interesting suggestion. Do you think he'll want to?"

"I don't know! Give it a try. Tell him that you'd love his help in getting one going, and let him choose what to grow."

She left with that suggestion, willing to try it. Six months later she called me back.

"Your suggestion was terrific! Lonnie has really taken to gardening in a big way. He is out there all the time with me, taking care of the things he planted. He loves digging in the dirt and has his hands in it every day, generally for a half an hour or so. We've grown tomatoes, lettuce, and radishes, and now he's into flowers. I can hardly believe it. He takes great pride in his achievement. Since he's begun working there his temperament has mellowed out considerably. He seems more *grounded*."

Even though he's still active in baseball and soccer, Lonnie's time in the garden taught him how to become quiet and connect with his spirit in a way that he loves. Now every time he gets upset about something, Diane finds him out there as a way to calm down. Using his hands, quieting his mind, connecting to the earth, was the perfect way for Lonnie to get in touch with himself.

CREATIVE VISUALIZATION

Another wonderful way to help your children focus inward and tune in to their inner selves is through a technique called creative visualization. Creative visualization is basically giving children positive suggestions through imagery. Because most children have such active imaginations and are so responsive to their parents, creative visualization is a very powerful tool for a child's contemplative life.

Have your children relax and get comfortable, preferably even lying down with their eyes closed. Once they are ready, speak to them very quietly and walk them through images that will calm them and give positive messages to enhance self-esteem and help them feel good about themselves.

I practice a visualization routine with both my daughters that we call "our inner journey." Every night after their baths and reading a book, when they're ready for bed, I have each one close her eyes and listen to my voice while I tell her how wonderful her spirit is and that she should think of all she is proud of. I ask her to remember her victories, forgive her hurts, let go of her frustrations, visualize improving those areas she wants to improve, and then peacefully go to sleep, knowing that God, her angels, and all of her family and ancestors love her completely. We vary the visualization from night to night. I give them each five or six minutes just before going to sleep. It's a form of healing that we look forward to sharing and is very grounding to all of us.

Anyone can do creative visualization with children. All it takes is a relaxed state, no interruptions, an easy tone of voice, and a heartfelt flow of loving images intended to calm and relax and affirm the worth and lovability of your child. In order to be in such a state you may need to do a little preparation, however. For example, it's best to do the "inner journey" visualization after a child has already begun to unwind a little. You can begin the unwinding process by having your child take an aromatherapy bath just before bed with the essential oils of chamomile, rose, and lavender added to the water. Two or three drops of this oil (found in health food stores everywhere) in a warm bath has an amazingly calming effect on a child's nervous system.

Tool CLEARING THE DECKS

One at a time, invite your children to share anything they want about their day without you "fixing" it, as a way of connecting heart to heart. Your task is simply to listen to them and not try to change anything. When they are finished sharing their day (which may consist of "dumping" their frustrations on you), ask them if they would like you to do anything for them. They may say yes and make a request, but often they will say no, satisfied with simply being heard. Once they've aired all that is on their minds, you can prepare for their visualization.

Tool INNER JOURNEY

Begin your visualization by dimming the lights and gently stroking your child's hair for a moment or two. Ask your child to take in a deep, cleansing breath and then exhale very slowly. Have him do this two or three times, asking him to imagine relaxing a little more each time.

Next, ask your child to remember all the things about his day that may have taught him something new, something he may have never before discovered. Ask him to enjoy for just a moment what it felt like to discover something new. Then give him a moment to reflect on it.

Next, quietly stroke his hair or back and ask him to focus on his breath, to inhale, and then gently exhale once again. After another twenty or thirty seconds, suggest to your child that he remember everything that might have upset him that day. Once he does this, ask him to imagine handing over all his upsets to his guardian angel to work on while he sleeps.

Tell your child that his angel will work on solutions to his problems during the night. Tell him that he can relax and not worry about a thing. He can simply sleep and refresh himself. Then once again remind him to breathe deeply in and out and to relax.

Finally, after another ten or twenty seconds, name everything about your child that is good and loving and true, such as:

"You are kind.

"You are intelligent.

"You are strong.

"You are intuitive.

"You are peaceful.

"You are loved and safe and important to the world."

Finish by saying, "I love you very much," and giving him a good-night kiss. My children and I call this "our special good-night poem."

This evening ritual is very healing and has become a central part of our family life. It takes only five or six minutes, yet the time spent is so effective in helping parents connect with their children, helping children relax and tune inward, and enabling both parents and children to feel supported by the Universe that it does wonders for the entire family. My own children get so much pleasure and nurturing from our "inner journey" that I even tape-record it for them to listen to on evenings when I'm away.

I've shared my ideas on doing a creative visualization, but only as a model for you to work with. Trust that your own words and images, particularly significant to you and your child, will flow easily and freely while doing the visualization. Be natural and allow yourself to be creative. When you do so the perfect images and words will flow.

A final word about tuning inward and the need for quiet time. Shut off the TV and insist on silence from time to time. We are so bombarded by noise that it becomes impossible to hear the soothing voice of our soul. The spirit is gentle and patient and will not compete with the outside world. Though tuning inward is natural, a little help from you in creating optimal conditions for supporting it is always a good idea. When it comes to tuning inward as a means of accessing intuition, don't get hung up on the method. Just get clear on the concept. Learn from your children and acknowledge the importance of connecting with the soul. Take a few moments in your own day and join them in quiet contemplative time, not as an assignment, but more as a gift to yourself.

CREATING QUIET TIME
Have your child:

> Sit quietly in a rocking chair and rock gently for fifteen minutes.
> Float on an air mattress in a swimming pool with eyes closed.
> Lie on the ground and watch clouds.
> Lie on the ground and count stars.
> Think of his favorite holiday before going to sleep.
> Imagine his guides.
> Lie on the floor and listen to Baroque music with eyes closed.
> Plant a garden.
> Work with clay or Play-Doh.
> Paint a picture.
> Learn to knit or build a model.
> Watch fish in an aquarium.

Reflections

1. What is your child's favorite way to "zone out"?

_____

_____

_____

2. What is your favorite way?

_____

_____

_____

3. Does your child have a favorite place to "zone out"? Do you?

_____

_____

_____

ART: THE SOUL REACHES OUT TO US

Because we are essentially spiritual beings, children begin life with a direct connection to intuition and spirit. They do not really have to _learn_ to be intuitive. They are intuitive naturally. They tap into this aspect of themselves instinctively through the world of creative play and spontaneous artistic expression. This is the domain of spirit. When children express themselves through artistic play, whether in dance, music, drawing, storytelling, or some other form, they are actually sharing the content of their intuitive and spiritual world. Unstructured creative playtime is the beginning of children's intuitive expression. All children are aware and have many intuitive feelings, but they may not yet have a linear, structured language to express them well. Even so, children can and do reveal these intuitive perceptions quite accurately all the time, through their drawing, music, and dancing. It is up to us, the intuitive parents, to recognize this expression as an important part of our children's souls. It is up to us to pay attention and see it as a second, perhaps purer language with which they can and do communicate.

I have worked closely over the years with intuitive and artist Julia

Cameron, author of *The Artist's Way*. She believes that "artistic callings are God's marching orders to bring beauty and soul into the world." Being connected to our hearts and giving expression to our souls puts us in a state of bliss. This explains why all children love doing art as freely as they do. It is a natural instinctive way to connect with their souls— that is, unless judgment and competition are introduced. When that occurs, the spirit exits and the ego takes over.

This is not to suggest that children don't need to learn to master their technique in art. In fact, any child who enjoys art enjoys mastering the use of the materials. But when mastery is emphasized over the pleasure of personal expression, when art becomes discriminating and competitive, a sensitive child's spirit can shut down and withdraw.

My friend Lu told how, as a child, she loved playing the flute. Because it brought her so much pleasure, she practiced constantly. By the time she was in third grade she was quite proficient, joined the school band, and was put in the first chair. In the beginning she was thrilled with this honor, but soon she began to encounter hostility and sabotage from the other flute players. Suddenly, going to band practice actually became psychically painful for her. She was glared at in the hall, whispered about, shoved in the lunch line, and so ambushed by the other flutists that she became very depressed. Two months of this was all Lu Ann could bear. She didn't want anything more to do with the "first" chair. She wanted simply to play the flute.

One day in band practice she moved voluntarily from the first flute chair, walked back to the last chair, and sat down. Greatly relieved, she sat back and waited for the others. Everyone in the band was surprised and confused to find that she had abandoned the coveted seat. When the teacher saw that she had moved, he asked her why.

"Because I just want to play the flute," she answered. "In the first chair it's too serious." And she stayed put. The other kids were surprised, some even acted embarrassed, a few apologized, and the teacher allowed her to stay in the last chair for the rest of the year.

Lu's story is more common than you may know. I am often alarmed at the amount of competition, ignorance, and snobbery surrounding our children's artistic expression. Such an ambitious attitude can actually silence an important spiritual language that our children require to tap freely into the well of their souls. Art is the primary language of the soul. Artistic expression in children should never have to meet a frustrated or ambitious parent's standards or pass competitive tests, nor should it be diminished as having no value by regarding it as only "play."

When parents have a denigrating attitude toward art, they influence children away from their connection with their inner spiritual world. Children feel this as no less than an intuitive amputation on the soul level. Such a severance allows intuitive disabilities to take hold and fester, often leading children to depression and even addiction.

I've had many clients come to see me for an intuitive consultation regarding their children's lack of focus or addictive behavior. In many cases of such general angst, I've noticed that the child is suffering a serious loss of soul due to having been cut off from artistic expression. These children are often the sons and daughters of well-intentioned, ambitious people who don't recognize the spiritual *value* of their children's artistic interests and so have discouraged them in support of more "serious" studies or athletic activities. These very children are so often the souls who have come to earth to help us all heal by giving us music, song, poetry, dance, sculpture, and all the other art forms that nurture our souls. If children perceive at a young age that their soul purpose and expression has no value, they withdraw, shut down, and seek ways to stop their intuitive pain, often dulling their consciousness with drugs or food addictions.

The best way to experience the value of art to the soul is to reconnect with it yourself. See it for what it is, the language of intuition and spirit. Can you imagine life without art? Life without color, sound, and sensuality?

Three years ago Patrick, the girls, and I had a taste of such a life, and it was eye-opening. We sold our house and purchased another, an old Victorian, that required a complete gutting and renovation. We then began looking for a temporary place to live during our project, which was not an easy task for a family of four and a dog. We rejoiced when we found a small two-bedroom apartment in the neighborhood, one that was rented to us very reluctantly on the condition that we didn't hang any pictures on the walls or change the "minimalist" decor in any way. We were so grateful to have a place at all that we did not anticipate that these terms would create any hardship.

We put all our furniture into storage, including our art, music, and family photographs, and kept what we needed to get by. We tiptoed around our rented flat in a state of anxiety, looking at empty beige walls and a tiny TV set. Our painfully extended renovation went on seven long months. During this time we gradually became increasingly depressed and irritable every time we walked in the door. Two of our baby-sitters quit. The girls' schoolwork suffered. I thought I had entered an early menopause, and Patrick was on the warpath.

It wasn't obvious at first, but eventually we identified the source of our poor intuitive condition. Sonia said it best as we spent one more evening under harsh lights and bare walls. "Mom, we have to get out of here soon. This place just doesn't have any *flavor.*"

We couldn't have agreed more. In our overzealous desire not to offend the owners, we had avoided creating any personal atmosphere whatsoever in the apartment, and we were now suffering terribly for it. Our spirits were indeed in need of flavor, the kind that comes from all spontaneous sensual expressions of the soul. No doubt about it, our souls were languishing.

The very day after we moved into our newly rehabbed house, we ripped through our boxes until we found what we were craving most. Our artwork once again up on the walls, one of Patrick's good soups on the stove, Sabrina's crayons and paints spread all over the playroom floor, Sonia banging on the keyboard, and my writing desk standing proudly—we *all* breathed a huge and grateful sigh of relief. In every sense of the word, we were once again *home.*

If you find yourself pushing your children's artistic interests too hard, or if you are impatient with your children's artistic efforts and want them to move on to more "serious" interests, ask yourself if perhaps you may have lost that sacred connection to art yourself. Maybe, without knowing it consciously, you have been cut off from your own soul food as a child, and now you are standing in the shadow of your children's soulful delight, wanting in once again.

Know that living vicariously through your children's artistic interests or casting darkness over it will hinder their spiritual awakening, and it won't heal your old wounds, either. I believe artistic play and expression should be a family affair, one where everyone participates, free from censorship, in an atmosphere of love and a spirit of fun. No competition allowed.

This is the family atmosphere I was fortunate enough to experience. My father was a gardener, carpenter, and painter. My mother sewed, did photography, painted, and designed our home. And both of them *loved* to dance. Our home was in constant sensual motion. We grew up around dance parties with the hi-fi blaring. My brothers started a band with two playing guitars and the other playing drums. My three sisters all sewed and designed their clothing, and I danced. Today, all seven of us are in artistic and creative professions. I have two siblings who are interior designers and one who designs furniture. I have one who is a computer graphics artist and one who is an intuitive healer, and I do intuitive readings. Above all, we are all connected with our intuition and have followed our hearts' desire all along. I believe our connection to art kept us in touch with our souls and our true sense of the purpose of life.

My teacher Charlie Goodman put it beautifully when he said: "Sonia, there are many ways to listen and hear the voice of your soul—through meditation, prayers, contemplation, even work at times. But if all else fails, connect with your spirit by using your hands. Be creative. The hands are connected to the heart, and the heart is the seat of the soul. The hands will always take you home."

Tool GETTING TO THE HEART THROUGH ART

Paint a picture.
Write a fairy tale.
Play with clay.
Sing a song.
Dance to your favorite music.

Play the piano.
Make a collage.
Design an outfit.
Invent a recipe.
Make a mess.
Do all the above with your children.

Reflections

1. What are your favorite artistic interests or activities?

_____

_____

_____

2. What are your children's favorite artistic interests or activities?

_____

_____

_____

3. Do you have a place in the house for your child to be creative and artistically experimental? For you to be artistically creative and experimental? Where?

_____

_____

_____

4. Do you or your children set aside any time in the day to work on creative projects? When?

_____

_____

_____

5. Can you and your children pursue art without having to be "good" at it?

_____

_____

_____

6. Have you had any intuitive insights while working on your art? What are they?

_____

_____

_____

REMINDERS

Are you:

    Being respectful of all vibes, no matter how inconveniencing they are?

    Creating an atmosphere of wonder and discovery?

    Remembering to create quiet time?

    Expressing your soul through art and play?

TWELVE

Angels, Helpers, and Guides

Growing up in an intuitive household instilled in me a profound sense of confidence and security that I am grateful to be able to pass along to my children. It isn't a confidence that arises from an egotistical sense of "I can do it." Rather, it is a sense of relief, knowing that I *don't* have to do it on my own. I only have to do my part, and the Universe will meet me halfway with support, protection, and guidance.

This sense of confidence first given to me by my mother took on an even more delightful dimension when I began my intuitive apprenticeship with my teacher Charlie Goodman at the age of twelve. One of the first things Charlie taught me was the fact that the Universe actually provides us with a spiritual "staff," a group of spirit guides whose sole purpose is to assist, support, direct, protect, instruct, and delight us as we work to fulfill our purpose in life. He taught me that we all have different spirit guides for different purposes. They help us in our day-to-day lives as well as with our physical, emotional, and spiritual development. Their only purpose is to make our lives easier, more enjoyable, and full of wonder. There are several different types of guides, each with its own specialty, and we all have a "staff" of these marvelous light beings assigned specifically to us.

Almost every child has many encounters with loving spirit guides all the time. We adults have just learned to ignore them. Robin, one of my clients, told me about her encounter with her spirit guides as a child.

"When I was a little girl, I distinctly remember seeing two spirit guides in my house. They were both from India and were dressed all in white, kneeling in the hallway with their heads bowed and their hands clasped in prayer. When I saw them they lifted their heads as if to say they were watching over me, then resumed their prayerful position. I wasn't sleeping. I wasn't dreaming. I wasn't sick or hallucinating with a fever. I was perfectly conscious and wide awake. It was daytime!"

Her eyes were wide as she recounted her experience. "After I saw them I told my mother, and surprisingly enough she believed me, even though it spooked her a little. What do you think I saw?" Of course I thought they were Robin's spirit guides, and I told her so.

I asked her, "How did that experience make you feel?"

"Well, after the first shock of seeing them I felt happy and safe, as though I had an extra set of eyes watching out for me. I liked the feeling of their presence. It gave me a sense of companionship. I thought of those guides often—so much so that I learned to meditate when I was a teenager, and I've even studied the Hindu religion in some depth. It's helped me keep from being a nervous wreck in life, especially when I was a wallflower in high school."

Yes, they were guides for sure!

RUNNERS

We all have guides called runners to help us find things. These spirit guides are there for us when we can't find our shoes, our keys, our school books, a parking space, a seat at the movie theater during the first week's release of a hit movie, or anything else we need to find. Children love having runners because they are forever losing things.

A client of mine, Francine, called to tell me how much easier her life has been ever since she introduced the notion of a "runner" spirit guide to her son, Max, who is four.

"Before we knew about runners, Max was forever losing his belongings and I'd spend hours of my day searching for them. Whether it was his coat at school, or his shoes at a friend's house, or his favorite stuffed monkey just before bed, a day never went by that we didn't have a big upset and drama over Max's lost stuff.

"Then one day, after learning about guides, I told Max that he had a very special spirit guide who would help him find everything he lost. Max was intrigued.

" 'Really?' he said. 'My own spirit? What's his name?'

" 'You tell me, Max,' I answered. 'After all, he's your spirit guide.'

" 'Hmmm . . . Chester! That's his name!' Max announced without hesitation.

" 'Great,' I said. 'Now let's put Chester to work! Let's start by asking him to find your missing gym shoe, the one we've been looking for for weeks.'

"Max closed his eyes and said, 'Chester, take me to my shoe.' And off they went. He raced giggling from room to room as if on a wild hunt. After a fifteen-minute search, I heard him squeal with delight, 'Mom, we found it!' And he came running into the kitchen with the truant shoe dangling from his fingers. Breathless and triumphant, he said, 'Chester's real! He told me to look in my desk drawer and there it was! We got it!'

"He was so delighted with his find that he's been asking for Chester's help ever since. He still loses things all the time, but with Chester on the job, it's never a battle to get him to search for them. In fact, it's fun!" Francine smiled.

HELPERS

We also each have another spirit guide called a helper. A helper is a guide who shows up to help us on projects, and because our projects change, our helpers change, too. Older kids of nine and up especially appreciate helpers because this is the time in their school lives where they are beginning to be asked to do independent projects. June, another client, told me this story about her eleven-year-old daughter Marcy's encounter with a helper.

Never the studious type, Marcy was completely demoralized when she was given an assignment in school to write about the farming industry in France, a topic she had absolutely no interest in and even less desire to learn about. Watching her mope around and put it off for several days, June finally suggested to Marcy that she ask her helper guide for assistance.

"What can a guide do?" Marcy complained. "I still have to write it!"

"I don't know," June said. "Ask and see."

So Marcy asked, "If I have a helper, will you please *help* me!" and left it at that.

Later that afternoon June asked Marcy if she wanted to ride with her out to the airport after school the next day to pick up a visiting friend.

"Sure," Marcy said, relieved that her mother hadn't insisted that she stay home and work on her project.

A short while into the ride, Marcy turned on the radio and began tuning the dial, looking for something interesting to listen to. As she searched the airwaves she happened upon a French accent and stopped. She had tuned in to a program on National Public Radio, and just by chance the interviewer was talking to a group of French nuns from a monastery in central France, who completely supported themselves by running their own farm. The interview was fascinating, and because Marcy had just come from school and was carrying her books, she was prepared to take notes. At the end of the program the announcer gave instructions on how to order a transcript of the interview, which Marcy also scribbled down.

Her formerly dry topic now animated with real people and their personal stories, Marcy was completely engaged. She wrote a beautiful essay on the nuns' experience and got an A plus for her efforts. After her paper was returned Marcy remarked to her mom, "It's lucky that I happened to turn on the radio at that moment and hear that program, don't you think? Do you think maybe it was my guide, coming to my rescue?"

"Of course." June smiled. "And what a good job your guide did!"

TEACHERS

In addition to runners and helpers, we also have spirit teachers or guides who oversee our spiritual awakening. I believe the guides Robin saw as a child were spirit teachers. When I was a child I had many, many recurrent dreams of being in France and watching a stream of French priests circle me and pray for me. These dreams were fascinating, compelling, and very comforting. Subsequently I have spent a great deal of time studying religion, French, and especially medieval Catholicism and its connection to mysticism and spirituality. I'm sure these dreams were of a team of visiting spirit guides directing my path in this life.

HEALERS

We are also given spirit guides called healers. These guides help us stay healthy, balanced, and full of vitality. A healer is the guide who whispers in your mind, "Time to go to sleep now!" or "Better not eat one more piece of candy!" A spirit healer is also the guide who will come to a child in a dream and say, "I love you . . . you are safe," when her parents are divorcing and she is afraid and full of despair.

Healers comfort, counsel, and support our well-being. Once a client of mine named Denise called and told me the following story about her five-year-old son Brian's encounter with a healer.

Brian had developed pneumonia and was suffering a serious fever and deep-seated cough. He was delirious with pain and flopping all over his bed in great discomfort for hours. Denise was beside herself with distress and anxiety over her inability to calm her son down. Overwhelmed, she cried out loud into the night, "Healers, help me! Please!"

Several minutes later Brian's whole body started to relax and he seemed to have become focused on something in his mind's eye.

"Mommy, see the beautiful lady over there?" he asked, transfixed with wonder at whatever he was seeing.

Denise began to get shivers. "No, honey, I don't see her. Tell me about her."

Instead of answering, Brian seemed to be following the woman with his eyes, and apparently she was coming closer. He laid his head back, closed his eyes, smiled serenely, and said, "That feels good!" He lay quietly for a few more minutes, breathing slowly, easily, and deeply for the first time in days. Slowly he opened his eyes and waved good-bye, continuing to smile, his eyes sparkling. Then he closed his eyes again and fell into a deep, contented sleep till morning.

"I'll never know who or what he saw that night," Denise told me. "All I know is that within five minutes of my pleading for help, Brian saw something, and it calmed him for the rest of the night. Some might say it was only a fever-based hallucination. Maybe so. But I believe someone in spirit answered my prayer, and I'm very grateful."

JOY GUIDES

Another type of guide we all have is a joy guide. Joy guides love to cheer us up and lighten our hearts. They frequent somber occasions, such as wakes and funerals, especially when the atmosphere at such times becomes much too heavy, too painful, or too serious to bear. I'm sure you've experienced a visit from your joy guides, such as when you were in an overwhelmingly emotionally intense situation, like a heated argument, and all of a sudden everything about it suddenly struck you as funny and you burst out laughing! Or when you were at your first opera, and just as the heroine was dying, you cracked up. If so, you were tickled by a joy guide. They are child spirit guides who visit us when we need a dose of lightness, silliness, and comic relief. For example, have you ever heard a group of children laugh wildly, just to laugh? And the more they laughed, the more they made themselves laugh even more? Making you cut up, crack up, and act silly and nonsensical are a joy guide's mission. They show up in boardrooms and at funerals. They show up on school buses and during movies. They especially like to show up when you, the parent, are lecturing your child and looking fairly silly yourself. They tease, tickle, and above all, restore perspective. They visit often and leave their healing touch on all who are in need of it. Consider yourself lucky when a joy guide shows up. It's a gift!

ANGELS

All of these guides are benevolent spiritual forces lovingly coming to our aid and our children's aid with the sole purpose of restoring balance, providing direction, giving inspiration, and making us laugh. You can tell when you've been visited by one of your spirit guides because you will always feel somehow reassured.

Children also have angels who watch over them, and many, many children have wonderful encounters with their angels. Angels protect us and keep us on our path and out of danger so we can fulfill our life's purpose.

A friend of mine, Karen, told me a delightful story of meeting an angel when she was young. She said that when she had just learned to drive at the age of sixteen, she often tooled about her hometown of Baltimore in an old hand-me-down family jalopy. She pushed the gas gauge to the limit because, like many a teenager, she had the car but not the money to keep gas in it. One late foggy night, coming home from a friend's house, the car sputtered to a stop on the expressway while running through what she called "a really crummy neighborhood." She was out of gas. She started to pray because she was scared to death and didn't want to leave the car.

"Help me, God!" she cried to herself. "I'm in trouble."

Ten seconds later an old, broken-down car pulled up behind her and out jumped a wobbly old Asian man with a gas can in his hand. With a nod and a smile he opened the fuel cap, poured in the gas, and then put the cap back on. With another nod and a salute, he left without saying a word. As he drove away in his old rattletrap car, Cathy noticed a bumper sticker that read "Praise the Lord."

"He came out of nowhere, as though he weren't even real," Cathy said. "In fact, I'm sure he was otherworldly. After he left I turned the key and the car started up right away. I was so relieved, I cried all the way home!"

Kids, and especially very young kids, often talk to their guides and angels. When they play quietly, you may even hear them having very animated discussions with these spirit helpers, and if you ask them, they may tell you their names. Angels especially like to visit in the night, when children are afraid, and when they do see an angel, children are eager to share these profound encounters with their parents. Adults often dismiss these reports as fantasy, yet they are real and reassuring spiritual experiences for an insecure child.

For example, one day last year I was on a flight from Minneapolis to Denver, seated next to a well-dressed businessman and his six- or seven-year-old son. During the flight the man took out *The Wall Street Journal* and began to read, while the boy, who sat between us, began to play with some sort of electronic game. I leaned back in my seat, deciding to meditate for a while.

A short time into the flight the boy said to his father, "Dad, I saw an angel in my room last night!" Hearing this, I opened my eyes. Without even looking up from his paper, the father responded, "You were dreaming, son." There was silence.

A moment later the child spoke up again. "No, Dad. I was awake, and she was in the corner of my room just smiling at me."

The newspaper snapped. The father turned the page and said, "There is no such thing, son. You were sleeping." And he continued to read.

The boy stopped playing his game but kept staring down at it. He took a breath and gave it one final try. "Dad, it was real. I was awake, and she was very beautiful."

Now the father seemed annoyed. "Son, this is nonsense. Now if you put it out of your mind, we'll read a book together."

A puzzled look crossed the boy's face, as if he were debating. Then he said, "Okay. Let's read."

My heart sank. The little boy had just made a very difficult decision. He had had a wonderful intuitive experience, and he obviously wanted to share it with his father. Instead his father dismissed his experience without thought and negotiated the child into doing the same in exchange for gaining his father's full attention.

Together they read for a while. The boy was clearly enjoying interacting with his father, but eventually the man got up and went to the bathroom. While he was gone the boy picked up the electronic game and began to play once again.

Pondering how this child was being cut off from his intuitive life, I impulsively leaned over to him and said, "You know what? I believe you *did* see an angel!"

With that his whole face lit up. Then his father returned, and that was the end of our conversation.

What I witnessed on that flight is sadly very common. All too many times it takes only one dismissive remark from an insensitive or unaware parent to disconnect a child from his intuition and the loving support of his guides. As one woman put it, "If intuition is fire—my mother is a fireman!" An angel is a child's gift, and it can also be a gift to the parents as well.

Let me share an interesting experience my family had with my daughter Sabrina's angel. One day several years ago, Patrick and the girls and I were in Iowa celebrating the fortieth birthday of Patrick's brother, Gene. We had gathered together with about thirty family members and friends on an old farm in the country for a barbecue and campfire. It was October, and with nightfall approaching a chill had set in. A huge campfire was lit, and everyone sat around it and began telling stories. I was on one side of the campfire with Sabrina and Sonia (then four and five years old), while Patrick was on the other side. After a while Patrick pulled out a bag from the cooler and said, "Let's roast marshmallows."

Sabrina instantly shot up from her seat and ran around the fire to get to the bag first. As she ran, she twisted her ankle and began to fall directly into the flames. Everyone screamed. Horror overwhelmed me as I realized that I was too far away to grab her.

All of a sudden her body, defying gravity, spun away from the fire, as though she had been pushed, and fell to the ground. Everyone gasped. Patrick and I rushed to her. "Sabrina, my God, are you all right?" I cried.

"I'm fine! That guy saved me!"

"What guy?" I asked.

"The one who pushed me," Sabrina answered, puzzled. "There he is, see?" She pointed to the space behind the crowd. We saw only the darkness of night. Everyone was a bit startled, but I understood and started to cry. It was her angel she was pointing to.

Later that night as I put her to bed, she was just closing her eyes when she bolted upright in bed, eyes wide open. "Look at the sparkles," she cried, staring into the corner of the room. Her eyes darted about, full of delight. "See those sparkles?"

I turned and stared but saw just the darkened room. She sat fascinated for a minute, then said, "It's over. Did you see?" She was beaming from ear to ear. I hadn't seen, but I knew that that night the angels were working overtime!

My friend Sarah's daughter, Anna, who is three years old and fascinated with angels, was especially comforted by the idea that she could actually call upon them for added protection when she was feeling particularly insecure.

Anna was attending her first summer morning day camp and was adjusting rather slowly to being away from home. After a few anxious mornings, however, she found herself really looking forward to her days, especially once she knew the routine. All was going smoothly until one day she was told that the following morning her camp group was going to go on a field trip. Anna, like most three-year-olds, didn't respond well to any change of routine, so, not surprisingly, she reacted negatively to the idea right away.

"Mommy, I don't want to go to camp today," Anna said to Sarah as they buckled their seat belts and were preparing to drive to camp.

Sarah, a very intuitive mother who was sensitive to Anna's feelings, knew she was nervous about going on the field trip and this was most likely why she didn't want to go. Recognizing Anna's fear of change and new things, and intuitively feeling the trip itself would not be a problem, Sarah said, "But Anna, today is your field trip. You've been having so much fun at camp. Are you sure you don't want to go?"

"I'm not *sure* sure," she said. "I'm just afraid!"

Sarah thought for a moment about how to reassure Anna and help her overcome her fear so she could go on the field trip and enjoy herself, and then she remembered Anna's fascination with angels.

"Well, Anna, if you're afraid to go on this field trip, how about if we ask your angels to go with you and keep you safe. Would that make you feel better about going?"

"Hmmm." Anna thought about it. Then she said, "Yes. It would."

"Okay. Let's ask. I'll go first, okay? Angels, please surround Anna and watch over her and keep her safe while she goes on the field trip today." Then she turned to Anna. "Now it's your turn, Anna. Ask your angels to keep you safe."

Anna thought for a moment longer and then said, "Angels, watch over me and keep me and Mommy safe. The end." And she smiled.

"Okay, Anna, now that the angels are on the job, how do you feel about going on the field trip now?"

Satisfied that she would not be going alone, Anna said, "I'm okay now. I want to go." And when they arrived at school she ran eagerly through the front door of the day camp without a moment's hesitation.

For some the notion of spirit guides may seem a little far-out or may conflict with religious beliefs. Perhaps you have been introduced to guides in another way. Catholics call on saints and angels for spiritual help. In other religions, followers call on the souls of their ancestors to look over them and guide their families. Still others draw from the spirits of nature—the sun, the moon, and the wind.

Whatever tradition you draw from is the right tradition for you. The important thing to remember about spirit help is that we are not isolated in our life's journey. Each one of us is part of the Universe, part of the heart of Divine Spirit. We are loved and protected. The entire Universe conspires for our successful life's journey, and it is simply up to us to open our hearts and accept the loving hand of assistance.

The world can be a scary place, and kids of all ages are very conscious of the atmosphere of caution and suspicion that exists in these crazy times. But a healthy fear of strangers can sometimes become so big that it erodes a child's confidence. By adding guide protection to the equation, you can reassure your children that there are forces greater than themselves who love, watch over, and keep them safe every day. And when a kid has guide protection, his spirit begins to relax.

Reflections GETTING TO KNOW YOUR GUIDES

Your spiritual staff lovingly seeks to serve you. Talk to your guides, silently or otherwise, whatever works for you. Give your guides names or ask them what their names are. You will be surprised by what they tell you. Don't be shy. Ask your guides to help you in every way that you need help. Remember that they *want* to help.

1. Have you or your children ever sent your runner on a mission? What happened?

_____

_____

_____

2. Have you or your children ever asked a healer to heal you? Describe.

_____

_____

_____

3. Have you ever had a joy guide visit the family? When?

_____

_____

_____

4. Have you or your children ever had an experience with an angel? Describe it.

_____

_____

_____

5. How do you feel about having guides?

_____

_____

_____

6. How does your child feel about having guides?

_____

_____

_____

REMINDERS

Are you:

    Being playful, having adventures?

    Using your artistic talents?

    Remembering to ask for help?

    Getting to know your guides?

THIRTEEN

The Soul Is Eternal

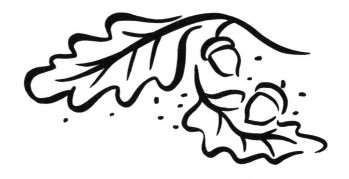

A few years ago a client of mine named Carla called me, very distressed over the recurring nightmares her daughter was having. Night after night, eight-year-old Ann woke up in a full sweat, screaming for her mom and insisting that Carla stay with her for the rest of the night with the light on. Exhausted by these nocturnal disruptions and not knowing how to stop them, she called me.

"What exactly is she afraid of?" I asked.

"She's terrified that we're going to die or something. I'm not exactly sure, because I keep telling her we're all fine and not to think about it. But it isn't working. She's obsessed."

"Well, that's the problem. Your daughter is beginning to be aware of death and *needs* to talk to you about it for insight and reassurance. If you won't talk about it, then she feels it must be even more terrible than she thinks. Her fears about dying take on a larger dimension than ever, scaring her even more."

"But I don't like thinking about death myself. It scares *me,* too. I simply don't want to know about it! Every time I think about losing the girls, my husband—especially my father, who's getting old—it's too upsetting."

"Well, Carla, it may very well be your fears that are giving Ann bad dreams. Your own aversion to talking about death can actually be causing Ann to intuitively pick up on it and overreact. These fears are manifested in Ann's dream state. It would be so much healthier for you both to discuss the reality of death openly and without fear, perhaps with a spiritual counselor or a minister." Carla told me that she had grown up as a Presbyterian, but she had left that church long ago, so I suggested that she seek out a new church, one that provided meaning and support, and speak to the pastor. It was time for an education on death.

My friend Lu Ann taught me a saying: "What you don't own will own you." The parts of life that are uncomfortable, like death or loss, need to be acknowledged just as readily as those parts that are joyous and happy. If you don't acknowledge sadness, you won't readily experience joy. If we don't prepare our children to deal with all phases of life, both joyous and sad, then when the wheel of life turns downward into death or endings, they will be overwhelmed and confused—or, even worse, they may even blame themselves for the losses they experience. Such self-blame is crippling to the soul.

MY SPIRITUAL BELIEFS

My own spiritual beliefs about death have evolved over time. They began at home with my very spiritual mother and continued to develop through twenty-five years of spiritual education, in part with my teachers, Charlie Goodman and Dr. Trenton Tully, and in part through my pursuit of religious, metaphysical, and spiritual study in school. Through this synthesis of influences, I have come to understand that although we have physical bodies, we are more than just our bodies; we are essentially spiritual beings. As such, we come to our earthly experience for the purpose of spiritual growth and creative expression. In order to do this, we assume a physical body so that it can provide a vehicle for our soul to achieve its goals. Not only does our soul take on a body so it can do its work, but it also chooses the family best suited to further assist its spiritual development. When we complete our spiritual plan for this life, the physical body, having no further use, dies, and the soul returns to the realm of spirit.

Because the soul's development is slow and difficult, it requires many lifetimes to learn its lessons. Therefore, once the soul has rested and reviewed the progress it made during the life just past, it elects to return to the earthly plane, enter another body, join another family, and continue on to another phase of spiritual growth.

As my teacher Dr. Tully once put it to me, "Lifetimes are like classrooms, with death being recess." He also taught me that our physical nature coexists in harmony with all of nature and that we are as much a part of nature as the trees, plants, and animals.

Understanding the cycles of the soul, I have come to see and share with my children how death is simply a natural part of the wheel of life. Perhaps your spiritual tradition is something other than my own. Perhaps you believe that the soul goes to heaven or simply dissolves into the heart of the Universe. No one living can be absolutely certain of the soul's journey after death. We can only intuit it. Whatever feels right in terms of your beliefs is right for you, as long as it provides comfort, solace, and hope for the future. Perhaps we can learn best from nature. Direct your children to notice the cycles of nature. Point out the seasons of birth, life, death, and rebirth. Explain that we too are part of that cycle. Children accept this very easily because it is natural.

Many people distance their children from the subject of death out of their protective instincts, but no matter how we try, we cannot shield our children from the fact of death. It's only natural that parents don't want their children to be frightened or worried or to go through the pain of loss, but in truth, children do have a natural wisdom and an ability to adapt to life's cycles if we will only trust and allow them to have an honest opportunity to do so. Protecting them from the reality of death cheats them out of the opportunity to perceive their place (and ours) in the larger scheme of things. In trying to avoid the unpleasantness of death, many parents lose touch with their children's natural and intuitive openness and underestimate how tuned in to the truth their children really are, even when very young.

DENIAL IS NO PROTECTION

Often parents avoid the subject of death with their children because they don't want to frighten them, but as my teachers have taught me, denial is not a form of protection.

For example, a client, Jenny, told me she had lost her father to cancer this past year. As hard as it was for her, she didn't want her five-year-old daughter, Shelly, who was very close to "Papa," to suffer through it as well. The entire time "Papa" was sick, she and her husband kept it from Shelly. As Papa approached death, they made up excuses not to take her to visit him, afraid that his appearance would upset her.

When Papa died, Shelly was told after the funeral that he had gone to heaven. Shelly was shocked and devastated. She was also angry and hurt because she loved Papa and he had disappeared into thin air. Worse yet, Shelly lost confidence that her family was safe. Since Papa disappeared so suddenly, what would keep anyone else from doing the same? She went into such full-blown anxiety over the possibility of losing her parents that night after night she clung to Jennifer, cried, or woke up with nightmares. Needing guidance in how to help Shelly, Jennifer sought help from her minister and learned that, all good intentions aside, they had made a mistake in not allowing Shelly to experience Papa's illness and death as a natural part of her life.

The minister explained to Shelly that it was Papa's time to die, that he had completed his earthly journey and his spirit was returning to God in heaven. When she understood that we all have a journey on earth, and that death is a joyous completion of that journey, she was able to accept Papa's death. Life and death no longer seemed so chaotic to her or so frightening. Though not fully understanding the wheel of life and death, Shelly at five years old could understand that the soul lives on and that each soul has a journey. Jenny and her family are now closer and more deeply comforted for having made the effort to grow in their understanding of what death is.

HEALING LOSS

Another client of mine, Rex, was extremely close to his grandmother, who came to live with his family when he was small and took a major role in raising him. He remembers vividly that when he was about ten years old he dreamed repeatedly of his grandmother dying. Upset, he reported these dreams on several occasions to his mother and father, but rather than talking about them and what they might mean, his parents dismissed the dreams as "nothing" and reassured him that his beloved grandma was just fine. Unfortunately, Gram wasn't as fine as everyone had assumed. Several weeks after this series of dreams, Rex's grandmother died suddenly of a stroke.

Rex's parents were in shock, and Rex was devastated. Although it made no logical sense, because of his dreams, Rex actually felt as though he were somehow the cause of Gram's death. He went into a terrible state of anxiety and depression, never talking to anyone about his fears that he had killed Gram. This anxiety festered for years.

It wasn't until he was an adult in therapy that he was able to discuss this childhood trauma and his terrible grief and guilt about it. With the help of an insightful and intuitive therapist he came to understand his dreams as precognitive. He realized that his grandmother's soul was merely trying to tell Rex that she was preparing to leave the earthly plane and perhaps to say good-bye. It took many sessions and a lot of reading on death and the soul before that dark cloud of culpability that had hung over him all his life lifted and Rex could heal.

I have seen so many clients who have inherited such unhealthy, undeveloped, fearful ideas about life and death and the nature of our eternal soul that it has actually prevented them from taking the kinds of risks in life that naturally go along with reaching our full potential. After all, life is to be lived, and how can it be if every step is taken in an effort to avoid death?

If you are extremely fearful about dying, then perhaps you may want to explore spiritual ideas concerning death that may offer you comfort and insight. Two of my favorite books are *Tuesdays with Morrie* by Mitch Albom and *A Year to Live* by Stephen Levine. There are entire sections on death and dying in many bookstores that may open doors to new and more healing beliefs than you now hold. You may also want to meet with a spiritual counselor—a pastor, priest, roshi, rabbi, yogi, or therapist—to discuss your fears until you come to some sense of peace. If you are actually facing imminent death in your family, through illness, for example, you may also want to contact a hospice center. There you will find profoundly caring individuals who will assist you in this transition with loving and spiritually awakened guidance.

IT TAKES TIME TO HEAL

Two years ago, the father of Sonia's classmate Kevin was killed in an auto accident. Though it was a terrible shock for Kevin and his two siblings, I was very impressed with how well their spiritually awakened mother, Noreen, handled the crisis and helped her kids sort through their feelings and attempts to heal. Instead of ignoring the situation, or trying to distract the kids from thinking about what happened, every night for several months Noreen gathered them together in the living room and encouraged them to talk about their father. At first numb, all they could do when asked how they were doing was say, "Fine." This lasted for weeks. Eventually, however, with persistence and gentle questioning Noreen began to help them process what had so absolutely changed their lives forever. At one point she told Kevin she wished his father could be at the upcoming baseball game, where he would be the star pitcher. At first he shrugged and said, "I don't care about him not being there." But then, a moment or two later, he burst into tears, screaming, "I hate it! And I hate him for leaving! Now stop asking me questions!" Seeing him cry for the first time since the accident, Noreen gathered him in her arms and let him sob. Relieved, she knew that it was his first step toward grieving.

Another time she asked Kevin's younger sister, Valerie, to get ready for church, and Valerie said, "I don't want to go to church anymore. God didn't help Dad, so why should I go? God doesn't care about us, or Dad would still be alive." Even Noreen felt the same angry emotions at times, and she knew that Valerie had to be angry before she could begin to heal, so that day they simply went for a walk in the park. As difficult as it was for all of them, Noreen included, they continued talking about it a little bit every day, until the kids felt comfortable sharing their feelings spontaneously. Some days there would be tears, other days there was anger. At still other times they reminisced about some funny episode they remembered with their father and laughed. Due to Noreen's patience and ability to listen and really allow the children to express their pain and sorrow, they were finally able to accept the loss and begin to heal.

Children need to learn as young as possible that to love and live life also means to expect change and even loss and death. I'm not suggesting that you dwell on this, but when death does come into your children's lives, be honest and fair enough to allow them to deal with it *in their own way,* sharing in their process rather than blocking it.

If your children have grandparents who are old or sick, let your children know that they may die soon. Talk with them honestly and encourage them to visit their loved one with you. Don't force anything. Death is *not* something to fear. Death is natural. When we remember that we are all soul travelers, and that our spirit lives on, these fears subside and we can then begin to accept death and heal from the loss it brings to us.

SPIRIT IS REAL

Some time ago I spoke with a client named Leah who had recently adopted a four-year-old son. Leah was putting all her energy into helping Douglas adjust to his new home when, out of the blue, her dearly beloved father died unexpectedly. Leah was devastated. Wanting to create a good home for Doug while her own world was shattered, Leah grappled with emotions that were pulling her in every direction. She spaced out a lot, cried at times, and couldn't concentrate on anything.

About two weeks after her father's death Leah awakened with a start to find Douglas standing next to her bed. "Mom, I just had a dream about Grandpa. He told me to tell you that he's okay and that he sent me here to be with you so he could go home."

"What?" said Leah, trying to focus. "What was that?"

"I dreamed Grandpa came to see me and said he's fine. He told me to take care of you," Douglas repeated.

It was an unexpected gift, a message from her father, and because of it she immediately began to heal.

THE SOUL IS ETERNAL

In awakening our children's intuitive hearts, we need to allow for all of their concerns, feelings, dreams, precognition, and intuition. These will inevitably involve both life and death transitions. We need to provide our children with a spiritually healthy framework to respond to these transitions easily so they can allow themselves to fully experience all of life's spiritual gifts.

Be open to responding to all of your children's intuitive feelings. When they speak of death, share with them what you feel. When they dream of death, let them talk out their fears. If someone in your family is nearing death, talk about it openly. Visit the dying person together with your children if possible, and urge your children to ask questions and share their feelings. Reassure them and let them know that death is natural and never their fault, and that the spirit in all of us lives on and remains in our hearts.

The more a family can identify with one another as spiritual beings instead of merely physical bodies, the more each member can relate intuitively to all that is possible and present in each soul, and the less frightening death becomes. This is the basis of a healthy intuition, knowing that there is so much more to who we are than merely the bodies we inhabit. Your children will sense this naturally. They just need to have it affirmed by you.

Tool LOOKING BACK

Together with your child, explore your forebears on both sides of the family. If possible, look at photographs of grandmothers, grandfathers, great-grandmothers, and great-grandfathers. Talk about their lives and what they contributed to the family that affects you today.

Tool THE TREE OF LIFE

Build a family tree on a piece of poster board, using family photos if they are available. If not, ask your children to draw their ancestors.

Tool IT'S ONLY NATURAL

Take a walk outdoors in nature. Search the ground for living things in various stages of decay and rebirth, such as an acorn that can come back as a tree. Help your children to notice the wheel of life, and point out to them as many ways as possible how we are all connected to the earth and to one another.

Tool CALL IN A SPECIALIST

Encourage your children to talk to their dead relatives and loved ones in their hearts and to ask them for support and love in their lives today. Talk about your child's various ancestors and their particular strengths and gifts. Ask your children which forebears may be best suited to help them with the challenges of life. For example, Grandpa the gardener may help your child with patience. Grandma the champion housekeeper could help with organization. Aunt Millie the artist could help with inspiration, and so forth.

Tool WE ARE ALL ONE

As you sit down to dinner, ask your children to notice where their food comes from. Show them how this food gives them energy and provides them with their life force. Ask them to bless their food and recognize how it supports their lives, and in turn, once they are fortified, they can continue to share this loving energy with the world.

Tool PAST AND FUTURE

Take your children on a walking tour of a graveyard. Discover who lived and died. Imagine who these people might have been, and invent stories for their lives. Invite the spirits of the dead to tell you their stories and to share with you their contributions to the earth. Now imagine the descendants of these people and what they might be like today.

Next, imagine that these souls have each come back to a body and are living new lives. What would their lives be like? Enjoy this exercise and let your imaginations run wild.

Tool BE THERE

Visit a relative or friend who is aging or sick. Don't be afraid to ask that person what it is like to be in his place and how you can best help him during this time.

Reflections

I. Who is your favorite ancestor?

_____

_____

_____

2. Who is your child's favorite ancestor?

_____

_____

_____

3. Imagine the future generations of your family. Invent who they are and what they might be like.

_____

_____

_____

4. Invite your child to notice and share as many examples of the wheel of life as possible. Give some examples.

_____

_____

_____

5. Write about your own connection with your children—past and future. Let your spirit guide you in this exercise.

_____

_____

_____

6. Have you talked with your children about death? How do they feel about it?

_____

_____

_____

7. Is anyone in your family sick, aging, or dying? How do you feel about this?

_____

_____

_____

8. Do you openly speak about the deceased person?

_____

_____

_____

9. Have you allowed the spirits of the deceased to continue contributing to your lives?

_____

_____

_____

REMINDERS

Are you:

Remembering to ask for help?

Getting to know your guides?

Remembering to create quiet time?

Aware of your eternal nature?

Epilogue THE NATURAL PLAN

One thing you will discover when you begin to nurture intuition, both in yourself and in your children, is that what you are truly doing is nurturing your most authentic self, your spirit. Nurturing intuition is actually the art of discovering and honoring who you really are. Being intuitive means looking into your heart and recognizing the genuine self within. Raising your children to be intuitive means empowering them with the understanding that they are spiritual beings, royal children of the light, thus keeping them from the darkness and confusion of searching for their self-worth through the approval of others.

It will teach them to view the world through creative and receptive eyes, knowing that the Universe is helping them succeed behind the scenes in every way. When we see ourselves as we really are, spiritual beings, helped by guides, protected by angels, and infinitely loved by God, then being intuitive begins to make sense. The Universe is a hologram, aware of all of its parts at all times, and each one of us, being an essential part of the whole, has access to its wisdom at every moment.

Being intuitive means being in tune with the true nature of the Universe, including your place in it, and will prevent you and your children from believing anything less than the truth: that as children of God, you are lovable and worthy of everything good the Universe has to offer. It will free all of you from the tendency to harm or repress your genuine needs, feelings, and desires. In living an intuitive life, you live with an open heart. In other words, you become committed to loving yourself and agree to accept the love and abundance that the Universe wants you to experience.

Teaching your children to follow their intuition will also help them to walk away from people or situations that are not good for them. It will let them know that they have the right to keep themselves out of harm's way by respecting their natural boundaries and identifying and moving away from negative circumstances without having to justify their reasons.

Being intuitive offers your children a world that is friendly, adventurous, and amusing, but most of all one that welcomes their unique essence. It will lay the foundation for their ability to experience real power in their lives, the power that comes from within and cannot be diminished by anyone.

Your children will learn the truth about their intuitive nature from you. Know who you really are, and above all, be yourself. No matter what, never forget that the children who have come into your life, no matter how, chose *you* to guide their way. Take whatever suggestions from this book feel right to you and ignore the ones that don't. You are naturally the best and most qualified person in the world to know intuitively what is right and true for you and your child.

Take hold of your own natural organic wisdom. Leave your fears behind and center your full awareness on your heart. Seek counsel and guidance whenever you deem it necessary for your children, but always put this counsel to the vibe test. And remember: Don't surrender your natural wisdom, even in the face of the most daunting authority.

Reclaiming your sixth sense and restoring it to its rightful place of honor in your children's lives will give them an invaluable gift. It will make them aware of the wonder in the world. It will open their eyes and ears to the glory and delight of creativity. It will arm them with confidence and provide added insurance for protection. It will help them connect to their real purpose and to those with whom they share their lives. It will assure them of their natural place in the wheel of life and help them overcome the fear of death. Above all, it will give them the right to live in peace without fear and to have the full experience of expressing who they really are. For each of us who lives with this wisdom in our hearts helps those who have lost their way remember their true essence as well. In this way we can all become healers of the world and usher in an age of peace. This is the natural way, and as it should be.

It is my hope that you, and they, will live intuitively ever after.

God bless,
Sonia
CHICAGO, JUNE 1998

Index

Nightingale Conant

*L*et Sonia Choquette help you tap your own guiding inner voice!

Creating Your Heart's Desire
Principles for Living the Life You Really Want

by Sonia Choquette

We all hold wishes and hopes for our lives—a nicer home, warm, loving relationships, financial stability. But too often our "heart's desires" go unanswered. We let fear and uncertainty hold us back from realizing and living our dreams.

But the fact is, you can channel the powers of your will and imagination to create anything you want! Now you can learn this incredible process and put it to work in your daily life with *Creating Your Heart's Desire*, a life-changing new program by internationally renowned intuitive and spiritual consultant Sonia Choquette.

The First Step in the Dance to Your Dreams

Creating Your Heart's Desire introduces you to the nine steps in the process of creative manifestation and shows you how to use them to bring all your desires into being. With personal anecdotes and real-life examples, Sonia demonstrates the infallible power of these principles to dramatically change your life. Once you put them into practice, you will be amazed at the power you have to control and determine events. Become the architect of your own glorious future!

6 Audiocassettes, Workbook, 5 Heart's Desire Cards, Principles Card, Instruction Card, Alchemy Box, Stickers, plus Candle　**18790A　$59.95**
First-time customer price $39.95

Your Psychic Pathway
Listening to the Guiding Wisdom of Your Soul

by Sonia Choquette

Imagine what it would be like to live without one of your senses—sight, hearing, touch, taste, or smell. Inside, we all have an extra sense that, used daily, will lead us to better decision-making and wiser choices. This sense is called the "psychic sense." It's what gives you gut feelings and alerts you to good or bad situations. When you don't use your psychic sense, it's like deliberately cutting off your sight, hearing, touch, taste, and sense of smell.

Reclaim This Amazing Piece of Natural Power: Your Psychic Sense

Your psychic sense is the direct line to your Higher Self. And when you activate this sense, the answers to life's most important questions will come to you with astonishing accuracy. Now with the help of Sonia Choquette, teacher, best-selling author, and personal consultant, you can learn to fully appreciate and make use of this power. You'll learn how to access your inner voice and use it every single day, for everything from where to find your keys ... to finding your purpose in life!

6 Audiocassettes, Special Journal, Workbook, plus Psychic Pendulum　　　**17480A　$59.95**
First-time customer price $39.95